MATCH
OF MY LIFE

Eighteen stars relive their greatest games

pitch

MATCH
OF MY LIFE

Eighteen stars relive their greatest games

Southampton

Joe Batchelor & Alex Crook

First published by Pitch Publishing, 2014

Pitch Publishing
A2 Yeoman Gate
Yeoman Way
Durrington
BN13 3QZ
www.pitchpublishing.co.uk

A CIP catalogue record is available for this book from the British Library.

ISBN 978-1-90962-650-8

Typesetting and origination by Pitch Publishing

Printed in Great Britain

Contents

Acknowledgements

Alex:

I'd like to thank Joe for letting me gate-crash his project, Emma Allen for painstakingly proofreading each chapter, David Armstrong and Francis Benali for helping put us in contact with many of their former team-mates and Pat Symes for sharing his wealth of book writing knowledge.

I would also like to thank my wife Lynn and my wonderful children Annabelle, Jamie and Oscar for putting up with my moments of stress as we were nearing the publication deadline and their unwavering support.

Finally, to my beloved dad Richard who gave me the inspiration to follow my dream of becoming a sports writer in the first place.

Joe:

Firstly, thanks to Paul Camillin at Pitch Publishing for giving us the chance to write this book. I initially thought he was joking when he mentioned it to me while having a chat on his doorstep!

Thanks to every player we have interviewed as they could not have been more generous with their time and went out of their way to assist us and Lawrie McMenemy for penning the Foreword.

Tim Manns at the ex-Saints association and Gordon Simpson at the *Daily Echo* for helping with numbers and Alex for taking a punt on me in the first place and allowing me to cover Saints.

Last but not least, this is for my parents Neil and Judy and sisters Catherine and Zoe, who supported me from day one when I said I wanted to be a sports journalist.

Foreword

Lawrie McMenemy
Thursday 28 August 2014

LOOKING AT the list of legends who have been connected with this wonderful club over a long period of time, it is fantastic the number of great players who have pulled on the Southampton shirt.

The names featured in this book cover every era going right back to Cliff Huxford in the 1960s, include internationals from more than one country and people who have played in World Cups and domestic cup finals.

One would automatically assume their greatest achievement would be playing for their country or stepping out at Wembley for the first time but often, when you speak to players, their most memorable or exciting time is something completely different.

That is illustrated by the match each individual has chosen. In some cases they have picked their first-team debut, a game in which they scored a significant goal or famous victory against one of the elite teams.

Like my FA Cup winning captain Peter Rodrigues, my favourite memory from my time at Southampton is the 1976 final.

It is a long-lasting achievement. I was at an airport in Florida a few weeks ago and a couple approached me to talk about it because they were avid Manchester United fans.

For weeks after we won the postman used to deliver a van filled with sacks of mail and presents to the club. I was sent an eight-foot long spear from New Zealand, a boomerang from Australia and a Sheikh's head-dress.

I met Roberto Martinez, the former Wigan boss, at a League Managers' Association dinner and he was gutted because they had just been relegated from the Premier League the week after beating Manchester City at Wembley.

I said to him, 'In 20 years' time when you are walking around Wigan all they will be talking to you about is winning the FA Cup.' They still stop me and it has been nearly 40 years. That is the magic of the cup.

That game was watched by every country in the world and put Southampton on the football map. I am delighted many of the players you will read about across these pages helped to build on that legacy.

The other significant thing about a lot of the older players featured is they used to play 60-odd games a season, people like David Armstrong hardly ever sat out a match in his entire career.

My cup final winning squad was made up of just 13 players and they only missed a game if they were injured. In those days if you left a big name out they would be banging on the door wanting to know why.

Three years after winning the FA Cup we also reached the League Cup Final, losing 3-2 to Brian Clough's Nottingham Forest.

That game was a bonus match for someone like Alan Ball, because he was coming to the end of his career and thought his days of playing at Wembley were over.

During my time in charge we also qualified for Europe and won promotion to the old first division, thanks to the likes of Mick Channon, who was a great player, and Bally.

Channon himself admits it was a hard task for me managing so many big egos and some strong characters have passed through the doors.

In truth the international players were the easy ones; it was the ones who thought they should be internationals who caused the most problems.

You will read first-hand accounts from Nick Holmes, Armstrong and Steve Moran who were all part of the team that finished second in the top flight in 1984.

That was a remarkable achievement because you need a bit of luck to win the cup but being the second best team in the country, behind the mighty Liverpool, over the course of a season is a lot more difficult.

It also fills me with pride that I played a key role in bringing through many of the young stars who are featured reminiscing about their early days in a Saints shirt when I started off what is now known as the academy.

I opened a stand at Gateshead athletics stadium for my friend Brendan Foster, the brilliant Olympic long distance runner, and I noticed there was a big warm-up area gymnasium.

I hired it for two nights a week and got the former Sunderland goalkeeper Jimmy Montgomery, Tommy O'Connor, who I played in the north east, and Jack Hixon, who had been working for Burnley, and his two assistants to find the best youngsters in the north east and coach them there.

In the school holidays they sent the best ones down to us for me and my staff to look at and that is how we discovered Alan Shearer.

Shearer played for the famous Wallsend Boys Club and there was a day when Newcastle United brought a load of trialists in for a game to see what they were like.

There was only one goalkeeper so Shearer stuck his hand up to go in net because he thought he would be guaranteed a game. He was useless in goal and Newcastle never took him on.

Luckily, Jack had seen him before and rang me and convinced me to sign him and Newcastle eventually ended up paying Blackburn £15m for a player they could have had for nothing.

I did the same with a bloke called Bob Higgins in London and that is where the Wallace brothers, Rod, Danny and Raymond, Steve Williams and Austin Hayes came from.

We also set up a youth centre in the West Country, which many years after I had left the club helped unearth Jason Dodd and later Gareth Bale.

Bally called it 'Lawrie's conveyor belt' because they didn't all make it and some fell off but it is a tradition that has continued to this day.

Matt Le Tissier was a different kettle of fish because we did not have a centre in the Channel Islands.

His move came about when a group of schoolkids from Guernsey came over to visit and one of the teachers called me to say they were being given a tour around Portsmouth. I said, 'That won't take long so tell the coach driver to bring them over here when they are done.'

We showed them around The Dell, took them in the gym, let them have a kick around on the pitch and served up some tea and cake.

At the end of the trip the teacher who was in charge was so grateful he wrote to me asking what the school could do in return. I said, 'If you get any special kids let me know.'

Two came over, Le Tissier and Graham Le Saux. Channel Islanders apparently get very homesick and as a result Le Saux did not want to join us then but I got Matty signed up.

At Southampton I had a theory of 'old heads, young legs' because the players I signed like Peter Osgood, Ball and the like you could not afford to buy in their prime, so you needed the right mix of youth and experience.

Those players were in the twilight of their career but as they helped us become more successful I was able to sign players like Kevin Keegan and Peter Shilton, who were both current England internationals when we got them from Hamburg and Nottingham Forest.

I remember when I signed Keegan I did not tell anybody in case any other clubs came sniffing around. You could not do that now because everybody has got phones and cameras.

There are not many players you will read accounts from who I did not cross paths with either as manager or when I returned to the club as director of football in the 1990s.

Claus Lundekvam and Egil Ostenstad were two of three Norwegian players we tried to sign when Graeme Souness was at the helm.

The third was Tore Andre Flo who went on to score goals in the Premier League for Chelsea and Leeds United.

At the time we could not get Flo but Lundekvam and Ostenstad more than repaid the money we shelled out on them. Claus, in particular, was a terrific servant. I also remember visiting Franny Benali's house off The Avenue when he was a schoolboy centre-forward and we turned him into a full-back. He is a legend with the public and, with due respect, not because of his natural ability like Le Tissier, but because of his 110 per cent effort.

Franny had a terrific attitude for defending and did not want anyone to get past him. The crowd appreciated that and loved him for it.

Nick Holmes – who is also interviewed – was a quiet lad. Nick could play anywhere and at times I used to use him in a back three behind as a sweeper, long before it was fashionable.

When I first came to Southampton after winning championships with Doncaster Rovers and Grimsby Town I never imagined I would still be living here all these years later.

Following a legend like Ted Bates, who had been manager for 18 years, was not easy and we got relegated in my first season, the first team to go down after finishing third from bottom.

If that happened now I would have been out of the door, but luckily the board gave me enough time to turn things around.

There was also the issue with moving from the north east to down south and where I came from I thought everybody here talked like Cockneys so that was a bit of a culture shock for me, but one I soon got used to.

My kids were bought up here and it is a good area. It has been good to me and my family and the club is an integral part of the community.

One of the things I always told the players before a game was how important it was to win, not just for the supporters but for the whole city because everybody benefits. I met a local businessman once and he told me if Saints win his sales go up and on a Saturday night the bars and restaurants are heaving because if you are winning more people come out to celebrate, and on Mondays the workers are more cheerful.

I used to insist the players got involved in local charity work and at the end of a training session I would say to the big names, Ball, Keegan, Channon and Shilton, 'Stay behind I have some kids coming to the training ground.'

Bally would put the goalie gloves on, diving the wrong way in the mud to make sure the youngster's ball would end up in the corner. The players would carry the kid around on their shoulders and he would never forget that moment.

I stayed in the area when I left and went to Sunderland, which was a bad move and a big mistake but the plan was always to stay in Southampton.

When I was working with Graham Taylor and England it did not matter where I was and when I was Northern Ireland manager it worked well because I could hop on a plane over to Belfast and most of our players were playing in this country anyway.

It also meant I could stay in touch with what was happening at Saints and have enjoyed many a day out watching the likes of Theo Walcott and Rickie Lambert, who is a top lad.

The nice thing about Southampton is the players who have turned out for the club down the years have always been terrific characters and I hope you enjoy reading their stories as they all have fond memories, as I do, of their time here.

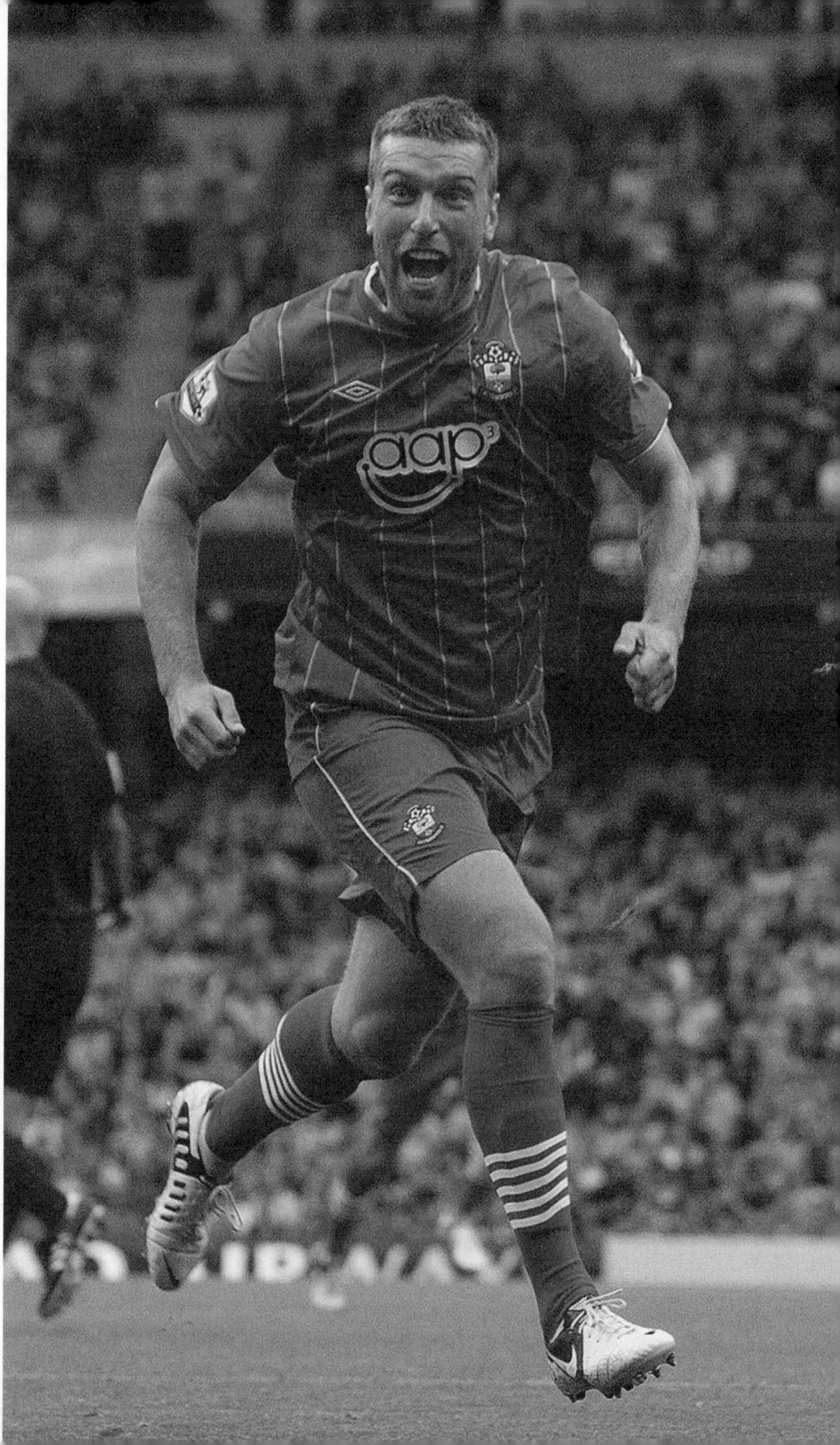

RICKIE LAMBERT

Rickie Lambert

Manchester City 3 (Tevez, Dzeko, Nasri)

Southampton 2 (Lambert, S Davis)

Premier League
The Etihad Stadium, Sunday 19 August 2012

Southampton: K Davis, Clyne, Hooiveld, Fonte, Fox, Schneiderlin, Ward-Prowse (S Davis, 65), Puncheon (Sharp, 86), Lallana, Guly, Rodriguez (Lambert, 55)

IT IS fair to say my first game as a Premier League player was one of mixed emotions.

It was the moment I had waited all my life for, so not being picked in the starting line-up was a massive shock. I was devastated.

I had trained all summer and was desperate to play. Mine had been a slow rise to the top and I had got myself in the best shape of my career only to find I was on the bench.

I remember Nigel Adkins pulling me to one side the day before and telling me he had chosen to go with Guly do Prado, our Brazilian striker.

He said it was a purely tactical decision and he thought because of my lack of pace I was not the right option.

Guly obviously possessed more pace than me and Nigel thought he could use that to isolate Vincent Kompany.

I had an inkling anyway as the manager used to set the team out in training on the Friday morning and I was put on the opposite side to what I thought would be the first XI.

I always respect the manager's decision but this was the hardest one I have ever had to accept.

I knew it was the Premier League and I would not be starting every game, but I thought after everything I had done to get the club there and all the goals I had scored the previous season I deserved to play in the first match.

I said what I had to say to Nigel. We had words about it and then I had to get my head right, ready to make an impact because I knew I was going to come on as substitute.

I also knew we could have been two- or three-nil down by the time I got on because City had hammered a few teams the season before when they had won the title with virtually the last kick.

To be fair to the lads who did make Nigel's team sheet they did terrifically and it was only 1-0 when I finally got the nod, Carlos Tevez scoring five minutes before half-time after beating our offside trap and squeezing his shot in at the near post.

In my younger days I was terrible at watching games from the bench and did not focus as much as I did if I was starting.

But in the latter years of my career I became a lot more professional at getting my head in game mode, ready to get straight into the action if required.

I was called off the bench ten minutes into the second half in place of our summer signing Jay Rodriguez and felt alert and ready for that moment when the chance came my way.

I was made up with my first touch after coming on because I came short and managed to control the ball, hold it up and pass it off to James Ward-Prowse, all the while being put under pressure by Kompany.

I had a desire to play at the highest level that had been bottled up inside me for years and in the moment when I scored the goal I let it all out. It was amazing.

Prowsey played the ball to my feet on the edge of the box and I tried a one-two with Guly but the ball hit Joleon Lescott and rebounded to me. I knew as soon as it dropped to me it was going in, even before I hit the shot.

When the ball nestled in the back of the net and for a long time after I did not think that would ever be beaten as the best moment in my career.

I had scored a goal in the Premier League after so many years wishing and waiting for that opportunity.

The only thing that compared to it was coming on for England at Wembley and scoring against Scotland, which was just like a fairytale.

Joe Hart was in goal for City and came up to me after the game and reminded me he had played against Grant Holt and me when we were at Rochdale and he was on loan at Shrewsbury.

I said, 'I know. I used to tell people I had scored against you.'

That was a hell of a game actually because we beat them 4-3 and were 3-2 down with a few minutes to go. I scored two and so did Holty.

Joe was powerless to stop my fellow substitute Steven Davis giving us the lead soon after I had scored the equaliser and at that point I thought to myself 'What is going on?'

Davo broke down the left before playing a one-two with Adam Lallana and beat Hart with a great strike in front of our own fans just as I had done. Davo is a great player.

He defends and attacks and has qualities at both ends of the field. He fits into any position across midfield and gets on with his job.

He is underestimated by the fans and the media but he is valued by the right people; by the coaches and the managers and the players around him.

I can remember speaking to Mauricio Pochettino about him and he pulled a face as if to say 'What a player.'

The longer the game went on the more we believed we were going to win so to lose in the manner we did was heart-breaking.

We knew we would be under pressure but we gave away two really bad goals.

City equalised after a goalmouth scramble following a corner when the ball popped out to Edin Dzeko and he put it in from close range.

Dzeko had come on as sub early on after Sergio Aguero had been carried off on a stretcher and was not a bad replacement for the Argentine.

For their winner we failed to deal with a cross from the left and gave Samir Nasri too much space to run into our box and he drilled the ball into the net.

They were frustrating goals to concede because if they had taken us on and put the ball into the top corner that would have been acceptable, given the quality they had.

Even though we lost in the end it was still a great buzz coming off the pitch knowing we had competed so well against the best team in England and nearly beaten them.

We went into the dressing room feeling proud of ourselves and the performance gave us the confidence to go on believing we belonged in the Premier League.

At that moment we realised maybe it was not going to be as hard as we thought it was and that even with the money players are earning compared to what we were the gap was not as wide as people had made out.

I want to put on the record my thanks and appreciation for everything Nigel did for me as a player. To win two promotions back to back was an unbelievable achievement and something the players and fans will never forget.

Leaving me out was not the only surprise he had up his sleeve. We were all shocked when he threw Ward-Prowse into the team.

Prowsey had trained with us all summer and we knew he was a good player but this was Man City away and managers didn't usually do that.

Fair play to Nigel for doing that because although we had principles at Southampton about bringing young players through, it was still his neck on the line. From that day the other youngsters have thrived because people like Luke Shaw, who was on the bench, had seen Prowsey get in and that gave everyone belief underneath him.

It was special seeing Prowsey, Shaw and Calum Chambers develop and that is full credit to everyone at Southampton.

Prowsey was only 17 at the time and I told him he was the exact opposite to me at the same age.

He doesn't drink, doesn't swear – doesn't fart – but he has a bit of character about him as well and I think that was massively important.

It was the same with Luke and Calum and I took to all three of them straight away.

Prowsey was famous for doing impersonations and used to do a great one of Nigel. The gaffer would have been horrified so he used to make sure he wasn't looking when he did it on the team coach.

Luke was not unlike me in that he hadn't been taught how to live completely the right way. I think it clicked with him at the beginning of the 2013/14 season and we saw the benefits of that.

My wake-up call had come a couple of seasons earlier thanks to Adkins' predecessor Alan Pardew.

I came to Southampton from Bristol Rovers and hit the ground running; I was scoring goals and doing really well.

I knew League One was below the level I was capable of and when I was at Bristol I thought 'I don't need to be in the best shape physically to score 30 goals.'

That was the mind frame I was in and, as a result, was not being as professional as I could have been.

Even though I was scoring goals for fun Pards pulled me aside about six weeks after I signed and said, 'I have been watching you. What the f**k are you doing?'

He questioned my professionalism, saying I was not looking after my diet and not working hard enough. He said I had another level to go to and said I needed to push as hard as I could to get the most out of myself.

I was a little bit taken aback because I had never been spoken to by anyone like that. I was shocked and embarrassed but knew Pards was right in what he was saying.

I looked at my team-mate Kelvin Davis, who was the ultimate professional, and saw the way he lived and thought 'I have got to follow that.'

That is when I contacted Nick Harvey, the club's fitness coach, and started doing extra sessions before and after training; gym, fitness, every kind of session you can think of.

It was about a month later I started to feel the difference on the pitch and that is when I thrived on it and wanted more. Since then I haven't looked back.

Before Pards had a word in my ear I was having takeaways at least once a week and when I was at Bristol six or seven of us players lived very close to each other and used to go out drinking at least once a week.

It was a very good group of lads and we were very close, which is why we did so well at Bristol Rovers, but in terms of professionalism it is not the way to go.

Joining Southampton was the turning point and it is not just what Pards said or the brutal way in which he delivered it, it is feeling the benefit of it.

For the first time I was as fit as everyone else I played against and that was a real shock because I knew I was better than everyone else and just went up a couple of gears and found playing games easier.

Had I not have changed my lifestyle I doubt I would have gone on to play in the Premier League nor represent my country at the World Cup.

The City game was also the first time we had tried the new 4-2-3-1 formation in a competitive fixture and I was a little disappointed we didn't try and stay playing the way we did in the Championship.

I understand it was a step up but felt we panicked a little bit at the start of the season, threw everything out and thought we had to do what everyone else was doing.

It took us a while to get used to the new system, with two holding midfielders, a lone striker and three players in behind.

At the time there was a lot of talk that the change of shape was Nicola Cortese's idea but I think it was Nigel's decision.

After the City goal I went on a good scoring run, netting in a dramatic 3-2 defeat at home to Manchester United and also in our all-important first victory of the campaign at home to Aston Villa.

The frustrating thing was when I was scoring goals we were not picking up many points and when my goals dried up we started winning.

At times in the first few games we battered the top teams and ended up losing in the last minute so it showed the character we had to pick ourselves up because people were predicting we would get the lowest ever points tally.

Attacking-wise we were free-flowing from the start but were not protecting our defence as we should have been and it took about ten games for us to click defensively.

We played QPR away and beat them 3-1 at a time when we were in the relegation zone and that is when I thought we would stay up because we were starting to become more solid and had stopped conceding silly goals.

By that stage I think the pressure of Cortese was getting too much for Nigel.

Nicola was a very ambitious chairman and had plans before he finally pulled the trigger that Nigel was gone but did not have a manager in place to come in.

Then we started to do well and Nigel still went after we had come from behind to earn a creditable 2-2 at Chelsea.

At the time I was very disappointed because we were beginning to pull clear of the relegation zone and I felt Nigel was guaranteed to keep us up so I wanted him to stay.

Mauricio arrived and I did not really know him but full credit to the people in charge who brought him in because he was unbelievable, a top class manager.

He, Mauricio, played the situation very well because he made an effort to get close to the main core of the senior players.

He bedded in well and made his ideas very clear. He was very good to me because I think he could tell I was a little bit uncertain and wanted to reassure me but it didn't take me long to be very impressed with the way he went about things.

There was a time a couple of months after he joined when the players were questioning his training regime because he worked us so hard.

Mauricio didn't like us questioning him and we had to decide if we were going to keep on moaning or accept it and believe in him.

We decided to go with it and from that moment we never looked back, avoiding relegation with a few games to spare before kicking on the following season.

Mauricio also played a big part in me breaking into the England team because it wasn't until he came in and altered the way he wanted us to play that people began to take notice of my technical abilities.

Even in the first season in the Premier League people thought I was just a big fella who scored the odd goal but that I was not good enough technically.

That frustrated me as well and I used that as motivation.

I knew I would have to go above and beyond to get picked by England. That was fair enough because it was my first year in the Premier League and anyone can have a few good months so I knew I'd have to perform on a consistent basis.

That was why I kept the determination to do well.

I remember a few games in that first season where England didn't have any strikers because Andy Carroll was injured so they only had Danny Welbeck and Wayne Rooney but didn't call anybody else up.

At that time I didn't think I would be picked any time soon but then a couple of squads later I got the call-up.

It was Mauricio who delivered the news on what was a very surreal day for me.

My wife had a baby at 6.30am, I got home at 8.30am and went back to bed to catch up on some sleep. I woke up about 11.30am to 25 missed calls and ten voicemails.

Mauricio's was the number at the top of the list of missed calls so I rang his secretary straight away and she said, 'The gaffer needs to talk to you.'

I didn't have a clue what it was about as I didn't even know the squad was being announced that day and he said, 'You have been selected to play for England.'

It was a weird feeling and my head was everywhere. I didn't believe he was telling the truth at first.

Another nice aspect about the club's first game in the Premier League since 2005 was that the bulk of the squad was made up of players who had helped us rise through the divisions.

From the first moment I joined the club I hit it off with most of the lads and knew they were good players. I am sure they will be the first to admit they, like me, weren't pushing themselves as much as they could have.

We knew we had something special and wanted to try our best to get out of League One and once we did that we wanted to get out of the Championship.

We managed to keep the core of the team we had and that is one of the special memories of my career, playing with the likes of Lallana, Morgan Schneiderlin, Jose Fonte and the rest of the players and working our way to the top.

There were some great characters who came in and out during the journey and I remember every single one of them.

Once we were promoted to the Premier League I started to room with Kelvin on away trips after my old room-mate Dan Harding left the club.

Kelvin was an oldie so was quite relaxed and liked to sleep a lot. He would go to bed about 9.30pm and start snoring.

He used to do my head in but was the best keeper I ever played with and as a character was exactly what I needed to guide me through those years.

He was brilliant and showed his worth at the Etihad by saving an early David Silva penalty after Jos Hooiveld had tripped Tevez.

I know Kelvin will be a good goalkeeper coach, without a doubt, but I think he can do more than that and become a coach, an assistant and even a manager.

Kelvin was always the most vocal in the dressing room and would organise the secret Santa at Christmas and chair the players' meetings every Friday when fines for any wrong-doing during the week would be dished out.

Whenever things were not going well and we had lost two or three games on the bounce we would have a meeting among the players led by Kelvin to work out how we could improve the situation.

Kelvin remained club captain but handed the armband to Lallana on the pitch.

It felt right and Ads thrived on the captaincy, although it came as a bit of a surprise to him at first.

When I praise Ads it is his will to win that I love and he is more vocal than people realise. When things were not going well he would hammer me.

I looked up to him even though he is seven years younger than me. He was a top class captain.

Jos was another loud character, funny with a weird dress sense. For a big guy he could bust a move on the dance floor too.

Our big Dutch defender would have been leading the banter in training in the build-up to our Premier League bow and there were jokes flying around that City would give us the run-around.

It was light hearted and we joked we wanted to keep the score down to five because there were a few nerves in the camp.

The coaching staff did very well in that environment to make us believe because it was a very intimidating time and we didn't know if we were good enough.

I remember when the fixtures were released a few weeks earlier and being excited by the run we had, with City, United and Arsenal among our early season opponents.

There was an immaturity about the league and that is the way most of us were at the time. We didn't care how good a team was, we were just going to steamroll them and go over the top. That is how we approached the Championship and we were going to match them.

It was very different because you could play well and still get beat three- or four-nil. If you were not solid you would get punished. It was absolutely ruthless.

A couple of weeks after the City game we played Arsenal away and lost 6-1. It was horrendous, one of the worst days ever.

Kelvin got dropped after that and it was difficult to see what it did to him. It knocked him and he was certainly not to blame. He even saved a penalty. We tried not to let that result knock our confidence too much and the fans played a big part in that because they stuck with the team, as they had through all our ups and downs.

I had an unbelievable relationship with the Saints fans and went through a lot with them.

When I played against them for Liverpool the first time after leaving it was special to see they still had that appreciation for me, and I will always have appreciation for them.

Southampton is a great club, a special club which will always be close to my heart. They gave me the opportunity to realise my dream of scoring in the Premier League, which is why I will always remember the game at the Etihad.

JOS HOOIVELD

Jos Hooiveld

Southampton 4 (Sharp, Fonte, Hooiveld, Lallana)

Coventry 0

The Championship

St Mary's Stadium, Saturday 28 April 2012

Southampton: Davis, Butterfield, Fonte, Hooiveld, Fox, Guly, Hammond (Cork, 37), Schneiderlin, Lallana (Puncheon, 82), Sharp (De Ridder, 76), Lambert

IT IS four o'clock in the morning before one of the biggest games of my football career and I am trying to get some much needed sleep. But, someone has rung my doorbell about 150 times.

Who on earth could be doing this at such an ungodly hour? And then it hit me.

As it was such a huge game I had a full house with all my family and girlfriend's family over to support me.

They had come over from Holland the day before as the chance to see me potentially promoted to the Premier League was not to be missed.

Everyone was excited about the game and it was nice they would all be a part of this special stage in the season. It was really nice to have them all over.

At one point though they decided to go for some drinks in Southampton and I obviously went to bed early to prepare for the game.

In true Dutch style, one thing led to another, and they went for a proper night out on the booze. First of all, my dad Aaldrik, and in-laws came into the house at a fairly decent time, around midnight. That was fine.

My brother Bas on the other hand decided to stay out a lot later that night and came home at 4am without a key.

You can imagine my mood in the middle of the night when I realised who it was. Only a few hours later I would be walking out onto the St Mary's pitch against Coventry with the chance to seal promotion to the top flight.

Before a game like that I don't really sleep very well anyway but this certainly did not help. It was a 12.30 kick-off as well so I could not exactly have a lie-in to compensate.

I went to open the door for Bas and then went back to bed.

But the ordeal was not over! My dad was a bit disorientated with everything and at one point came walking into my bedroom and asked where the toilet was.

That was at around 5am. It was a shocking lead up to the game and terrible preparation as I had barely had any sleep.

I was, understandably, a little angry at my brother and I had a few serious words with him.

I said, 'I can't believe you had such a big night out before a game which is so important for me.' We sorted it all out before kick-off though and I felt much better.

He realised he was in the wrong and apologised. Of course, everything was fine and I can look back and laugh now. As it turned out, no harm was done whatsoever and I capped one of my finest campaigns with my eighth goal of the season which helped us achieve our goal of going up.

The way we played under Nigel Adkins was amazing and it was great to be a part of. When I look back it is one of my favourite times.

It was also one of my best from a professional level. I had a few great years in Sweden with some nice individual prizes but if you look at what this season, and this game in particular brought me, then it is one of the most memorable I have been involved in.

In the week of build-up, all the lads were buzzing. We were in the zone, were going for it and had our destiny in our own hands.

I had been confident we could finish in the top-two after we had played 23 games and reached the halfway point of the season. As soon as we had played every other team once and I knew what we were up against I said to everyone, 'Boys, if we stay focused we can do this.'

And we could not have asked for a more perfect scenario to prove me right, playing a team who were going to be relegated on the last game of the season at home, which had been a bit of a fortress for us.

It was a great atmosphere with 32,363 fans packed inside which, at the time of writing, is still a record for St Mary's.

Despite being in the top-two from the first game of the season, West Ham were only two points behind us with one match each left to play.

Luckily, West Ham did their job by beating Hull 2-1 in a match played at the same time. I say luckily because I did not want to win promotion by default. We wanted to win it ourselves with the three points.

It had got a bit nervy towards the end and we had only won two of our previous six games with defeats to Blackpool, Reading and Middlesbrough.

The 3-1 loss at home to eventual champions Reading was a bitter pill to swallow as we battered them in the second half.

A long hard Championship season had come down to these 90 minutes. It is a division which seems to get harder every year.

That particular season 18 teams had Premier League experience which made it incredibly tough, it is one hell of a difficult league to climb out of.

Nigel told us beforehand to just go out and do what we had done all season, which was play attractive football.

He was nervous and under pressure to deliver promotion but we all had a belief our philosophy would see us over the line.

Nigel was very good to work with as he knew what the boys needed and was always enjoyable to be around.

We started nervously and Kelvin Davis had to be alert to keep out a curling left-foot shot from Gary McSheffrey which was destined for the top corner.

It would have to be something special to beat Kelvin that season, he was a rock for us. I vividly remember the 1-0 win away at Leeds when he single-handedly won us the game with a string of saves I didn't think were possible.

He was rightly named in the Championship Team of the Year, alongside Adam Lallana and Rickie Lambert.

I think Gary's chance gave us the wake-up call we needed and we soon settled down to get the opening goal through Billy Sharp after 16 minutes.

Billy was great for us and when he arrived in January it was just at the right time to help Rickie with the burden of scoring the goals. He found the net nine times in 15 appearances, a fantastic return.

Not that Rickie needed much help that season, he seemed to score every week. He scored 27 goals in the league and 31 in total. His record says it all.

He was unbelievable and with that tally of goals he was of course a huge part of what we did.

It was a nice surprise to see the quality of all my new team-mates, especially Rickie, when I joined the club. I was not aware of what they were capable of as I wasn't always following League One.

I don't judge anyone until I get to know them and see them play, that is a good part of myself and my way of life.

Rickie was amazing on the training field, in the dressing room and as a person. Everything was spot on about him. It didn't matter for me what standard he had played at before. It didn't matter if he had been in League One or the Conference. He showed me what he could do and that made my mind up – he was, and still is, a fantastic player.

Billy's goal in this game came when Guly do Prado sent in a curling cross from the right-hand side which Adam met with a crisp volley from 18 yards.

Being a typical poacher, Billy was in the right place at the right time with his predatory instincts to divert it past Joe Murphy and calm the nerves all around St Mary's.

Three minutes later the party in the stands really started to take shape when my defensive partner Jose Fonte sent a diving header from Adam's corner high into the net.

It was Jose's first goal of the season and I was delighted for him as he was desperate to get off the mark and get his goal.

Luckily for him, we did not have any bets with each other as to who would score the most. He would have lost big time!

They were two very quick-fire goals but even at 2-0 up we were still not relaxed. That scoreline is always a bit dodgy as Nigel pointed out at half-time.

If Coventry had got just one lucky goal it would have been squeaky bum time again. We had chances to put the game to bed long before we did with Adam having a shot blocked, Guly going close with a header and Rickie sending a fierce drive just over the bar.

Thankfully though, the next goal was mine and I can still remember it very clearly.

It came in the 59th minute when Danny Fox sent in an in-swinging corner that was not cleared fully.

Billy turned and shot with the rebound falling kindly at my feet and I whacked it in from close range with my left foot. Wow, what a feeling. It was amazing, spine-tingling.

As I have mentioned already it was my eighth strike of the season but funnily enough it was only the second to come on a Saturday afternoon.

Five had come on Tuesday night games, and one on a Wednesday. It was unbelievable and I still can't give you an answer as to why. It just happened like that.

The atmosphere under the lights is always amazing and the build-up to the games is also a bit different.

It is longer but also shorter in one sense as you go and have a little sleep and before you know it the game is there. If you play at 3pm you always wake up early at the same time and it can drag a bit.

I really try to help my team-mates out and score a few goals as it helps so much. You only have to look at our tussles with West Ham that season.

They were two very crucial games and I managed to score in both of them, once in a 1-0 win and then in a 1-1 draw.

When a defender scores from a set-piece or something it is certainly an extra help for the side and takes a bit of pressure off the attacking players.

It was a great sensation for me, knowing my goal had all but confirmed our place in the Premier League, a place the club had not had for seven years since their relegation.

We still had time to put the cherry on the cake and score the fourth though when Adam deservedly got in on the act with a neat side-footed finish.

Jack Cork sent in a deep cross which Rickie got above his marker to head back across goal. Adam sprinted in to bag his 13th goal of the season and make the ground shake once again.

Adam was a key player for us and really started to turn it on that season. He was one of the local boys who had done really well for himself. Some of the things he did were just unbelievable and a joy to watch.

The final 25 minutes were a procession for us but I still desperately wanted a clean sheet. Carl Baker had a shot which Kelvin saved but apart from that, we managed to see out the game comfortably.

There was a massive pitch invasion afterwards which was special and as we left the pitch being held aloft by jubilant supporters we could all start to take a moment and think about realising our Premier League dream.

As a young boy, it was a desire of mine, just as I think it is for everyone, to play in the Premier League.

I could not watch any games when I was younger as we did not have the channels that showed English football but players like Jaap Stam and Ruud Gullit were idols of mine and players I would look up to.

As was Ronald Koeman, who I was fortunate enough to work with later in my Southampton career.

It would definitely have been nice to finish first in the Championship and pick up the trophy but in the end we finished one point behind Reading. At the end of the day though, first and second is the same prize.

We had a great night at the Four Seasons Hotel to celebrate with the champagne and beers flowing. The day afterwards was good as well when everything started to sink in about what we had achieved.

The whole team then flew to Marbella and spent a few days together with everything we could possibly want or need included for us. It was such a great laugh and the atmosphere between the squad was unbelievable.

My dance moves would always go down well with the lads. I am a good dancer and showed Rickie some moves but he has such stiff hips he couldn't cope with them!

It wouldn't just be on team bonding nights, I would show my dance moves anywhere, no matter what time or place. After we won promotion I was dancing for the whole week.

The bond between the players was very evident when I first signed from Celtic on transfer deadline day in August 2011.

It was a tight knit group as they had been through a fair bit together already in being promoted from League One.

They definitely welcomed me with open arms and I received a lot of help from the senior players. It was something I would always try to replicate for all the players who arrived after me.

Kelvin, being club captain, was of course one of the first to reach out. We had Danny Butterfield and quite a few other older English boys who I instantly hit it off with which helped me greatly to integrate so quickly with all the lads.

It was very nice for a foreigner, like me, to be accepted by the old guard so quickly. If they accept you, all the others will. I felt involved and part of the squad very quickly. The people were all so warm and helpful. Everything was done for me and I didn't have to think much about myself, they helped me with everything so I could concentrate on football.

It would be fair to say I definitely found my home when I signed for the club. I had played in a lot of countries before and was very experienced but Southampton just felt right.

Initially I came on a four-month loan from Celtic and after three months I was delighted to sign on a permanent deal.

It was a slight gamble as I didn't speak to anyone before I jumped on a plane to head to the south coast. It was deadline day so everything was all a bit rushed but I had a quick medical and the deal was done.

Then I was introduced to Nigel and Nicola Cortese was also there to welcome me. I remember when I first met Nicola we had an instant connection and clicked straight away.

He told me about all the ideas the club had and he told me where the club would be heading. It was a very clear picture about what was going on, that was very nice and after that I had to prove I was going to be part of that picture.

I tried my best both on and off the pitch and would like to think I was a big influence in the dressing room and in training.

That is how I get the best out of myself. When you are one of the senior players it is important to be vocal and for everyone to know what is at stake.

If something needs to be said I would make sure my voice was heard. I would always be positive, nice and when things went bad, I would try to be one of the main players to try and pick everyone up and turn things around.

Off the pitch I think I played a big part in the whole season, as did a lot of the other players, including Jose.

I developed a strong partnership with him on the field and it did not end there. We had a fair few nice dinners with us and our girlfriends. Having a good relationship with the man next to you in the team helps and we were a solid team in the centre of defence.

It ran throughout the team that season and everyone got on so well, we were very close and a whole team of friends. I suppose it helps when you win as many games as we did.

What pleased me though was when we started losing games the following season in the Premier League we all stuck together.

I remember early on in our tough start to life in the division there were a lot of bad moments and the senior professionals had to step up and raise the spirits.

It was so important we did not lose the spirit and it was a crucial time for us. Once we got through the tough start we started to settle and do well.

I had no doubts players like our French midfielder Morgan Schneiderlin, Jose, Adam, Rickie and all the others could make it at the next step.

A lot of people can adapt to that level if you have a bit of time but that is the problem with the Premier League, you hardly get any time.

I always believed we would match the level and you can see it now, some of them didn't just match it, they went above and beyond it.

To have Manchester City away, Manchester United at home and then Arsenal away in your first four fixtures is never going to be easy.

You need to get up to speed, know what you can do and know your place. We went in a little bit naïve and tried to play them off the park like we did before and came up against a brick wall.

You have to realise to not go down this route but in a different direction. We adapted at the right moment and found our feet.

Nigel ended up leaving and I think it was the right choice. If you see what happened when Mauricio Pochettino came in that season and in particular, the one after, it was a very good thing for the club.

Look where we ended up, we had a record amount of points and that can only be a positive thing. The players also benefited. You just have to see how many players were called up into the national teams and players who have now left for big money.

One thing that is mentioned with me and our first season after promotion was that I scored three own goals, an unwanted record I share with three others players for the most in a single season in the top flight. It was unbelievable and really unfortunate.

They came against Arsenal, Fulham and Newcastle. It was just one of those things and something you look back on and wish never happened. You wish you were not at that place, did not stick your foot out and there are a lot of things that go through your head.

It was hard and the only thing I do regret from the whole episode is that I did not get the support from the fans I was hoping for.

I remember at one point after an own goal I got abuse and stick from a section of the Northam Stand and a few personal things written on social media and the internet that were hurtful. It didn't really help to be fair.

Of course, I should make it clear it was only a small minority but at one point I thought to myself that is not really the way they should have dealt with it. I did not do it on purpose.

But it is also a game of emotions and sometimes in bad moments people react in a negative way and I can understand that.

I guess I just thought after all I had done the season before I would have had a bit more support at the moment when things were not going as well.

It makes you stronger mentally now but at the time I wasn't thinking like that. Despite these unsavoury incidents I really had a great relationship with the fans and they were first class with me right up until the day I left.

It was the right time to move on for the next stage of my career. It was, of course, really sad to leave and as it all happens so quickly you don't have time to think about it too much and say all your goodbyes.

I will always be proud of what we achieved during my time at Southampton, going from a newly promoted side in the Championship to pushing for Europe in the Premier League was a great thing to be a part of.

I hope you enjoy reminiscing about this special day in April when we got promoted as much as I have. I feel like dancing just thinking about it.

THEO WALCOTT

Theo Walcott

Leeds 2 (Hulse, Blake)

Southampton 1 (Walcott)

The Championship
Elland Road, Tuesday 18 October 2005

Southampton: Niemi, Higginbotham, Lundekvam, Hajto (Delap, 83), Cranie, Belmadi (Kosowski, 68), Quashie, Oakley, McCann, Fuller (Jones, 75), Walcott

EVERY FOOTBALLER will tell you the memories from your debut live with you forever but mine was like a dream come true.

Scoring a volleyed goal under the floodlights at one of the biggest stadiums in England, does it get any better?

I can still remember pulling into Elland Road on the team coach with 19,000 people crammed inside the ground and thinking 'wow, what a place this is to make my first start.'

I sat next to Dave Prutton on the bus and had to have my wits about me because I had heard that if you fell asleep on the coach next to Dave you were in big trouble.

He would mess around, drawing on you or something like that. That took away some of the nerves before the game as I was more worried about falling asleep.

Of course I still had a few knots in my stomach walking down the tunnel but nerves are a good thing and they soon disappear. When I stepped onto the pitch I forgot all my nerves.

Sometimes you get days when everything good seems to go through you and that was one of those days for me. The slow defenders Leeds had might have helped me as well!

They had a strong side and went on to reach the play-off final, and were playing well having won two of their last three games while we were still finding our feet in the new division.

The home team started like a train and were ahead after only four minutes when Rob Hulse powered a 15-yard header from a Gary Kelly cross past our super stopper Antti Niemi.

We found Hulse tough to handle all game and the big striker played a big part in us going 2-0 behind after 19 minutes.

Shaun Derry angled a free-kick up to Hulse, who controlled it well before laying it off for Robbie Blake to blast past Niemi from 20 yards out.

We could have panicked and crumbled but the experienced players like Nigel Quashie, Matt Oakley, Neil McCann and Claus Lundekvam ensured that was not going to happen.

Five minutes later I got my first goal in professional football. Djamel Belmadi played a long ball over the top which Paul Butler failed to head clear and could only manage to head up in the air. I muscled him out the way and unleashed a shot on the volley straight at Neil Sullivan.

Despite getting a good hand on it, Sullivan could only watch as the ball trickled beneath him and rolled into the back of the empty net.

It was surreal and I wasn't sure what to do so just celebrated by running towards the corner. It wasn't a fantastic finish but showed my confidence to take it on the volley.

What a feeling. It took a few minutes to compose myself after but I soon switched on as we desperately needed to get back in the game.

From the moment the goal went in I was more and more confident. I had one shot that narrowly flew over the bar and then came close to beating Sullivan with a lob.

I had bags of energy and was playing with pure enjoyment and no fear and at that age you feel like you can run forever.

Sean Gregan paid the price for that, getting substituted for Matt Kilgallon after 56 minutes, as I was running him all over the place.

His defensive partner Butler even came up to me after the game and told me he didn't think he will ever have a harder game.

That was nice of him and he also wished me well for the future. He said he did not want to have any more 16-year-olds running at him with that pace towards the end of his career.

All the players were quite shocked to see my pace at that age definitely.

They were always asking me where I got my speed from and I would give the credit to my dad as we are from an athletic family.

People think it may have been difficult coming up against seasoned veterans like Butler and Gregan but I enjoyed it and wanted to get involved at every opportunity.

They didn't like to run in behind and towards their own goal, I always felt if I dragged them out of position towards their goal they will drop off and allow me to run at them.

As a striker you have to make the defender think at all times and I knew I could make it difficult for them. I did something right that day which was a good feeling.

Despite Eddie Lewis and Blake hitting our woodwork with free-kicks I don't think we deserved to lose the match.

After the game our manager Harry Redknapp and the coaching staff were very pleased with my display and said they enjoyed watching me play, which meant a lot.

Harry has gone on to say that my debut was the best he has ever seen, which is a huge compliment coming from someone like him who has brought through so many players.

It would have never happened if he hadn't had that belief in me from the start. I have so much respect for him.

Before my full debut I played 20 minutes in the match against Wolves on the first day of the season which was a nice touch.

It helped me get accustomed to a match day with the senior squad. I also received a great reception from the fans which has stuck with me.

The supporters all follow the academy and know how good it is which is brilliant. I received a great deal of backing right from day one.

Fans at any club like to see one of their own come through as a youngster and work their way up to the first team.

As has been well documented, everything moved very fast for me after that gruelling 3-2 FA Youth Cup Final defeat on aggregate to Ipswich in April 2005.

The home support gave us youth teamers the confidence to show what we could do on the pitch and played a big part in us surprising a lot of people.

I had previously become the youngest person to play in the reserve team aged 15 years and 175 days when I came off the bench against Watford in September 2004.

When I played in that game I definitely felt I could push on and go further but of course I was a little bit surprised with my rapid rise to the first team.

The same year I played in the reserves the first team got relegated from the Premier League and I think, not for a selfish reason but for the academy side of things, being in the Championship enabled me to get my chance sooner.

If they had stayed up I am not sure myself or Gareth Bale, who made his debut six months after me, would have got our opportunity so quickly.

When we went down it resulted in Harry giving us younger players the chance to come in and show what we could do.

I took my opening chance on the pre-season training tour of Scotland, just two weeks after finishing school, and never looked back.

Harry was unbelievable with me. He said to me before my cameo against Wolves to just go out and enjoy it.

I remember I had forgotten to put my shirt on I was so eager to get on the pitch, one of the guys had to grab it for me!

Amazingly, the eight matches we had played in the league before taking on Leeds had all ended in draws. Eight draws in a row, which is unheard of.

I think Harry was under pressure to change things and in training just before we went to play at Elland Road he pulled me aside and said, 'I am going to start you tomorrow, I think you should call your dad and let him know I am looking for you to play 90 minutes.'

He went on to say how well I had done against Wolves, how much he believed in me and how far he thought I could go but the main factor for me was that he had given me a chance to let my dad know.

That was really nice, I told him straight away and he got in the car and drove all the way up to Leeds. I know that meant a lot to him.

If he had not been there he would have been absolutely distraught so I am very thankful to Harry for that.

With me being 16 at the time for a manager like him to have so much belief in me was amazing. The match I ended up having against Leeds would never have happened if Harry had not shown that trust.

Maybe some sceptics felt it might have been too soon for me to be playing in the physically demanding Championship but it certainly benefited me in the long term.

I was scoring goals pretty quickly as well so I felt confident in my ability to play at that level.

Harry didn't worry about the pressure of putting a young kid straight in the firing line or anything like that, he put his trust in me.

That is what I needed to have, a manager who believed in me so much. It makes everything so much easier when you have that and allows you to enjoy the game and express yourself.

At that age you just play like you would in your back garden and have no worries in the world. It wasn't just him though but all the players around me in the squad.

It might have been a bit tricky for them to have someone so young in the team but they were all great and sometimes, I must admit, I got a bit of special treatment.

One particular episode I vividly remember is being scared to death Dennis Wise might end my career before it even started!

In training one day I kicked the ball aiming for a wall but completely missed and saw it fly straight through a glass window leading to the gym. Everything stopped and I was panicking.

You can imagine my reaction when Dennis came out with a face of thunder. He was in the gym on the bike at the time and when the window smashed he got covered in glass.

He had glass in his leg and everything. I had the split-second decision as to own up or not. I did and when I said it was me to my complete surprise he said, 'don't worry about it Theo, it's fine'.

What a relief! I thought 'thank God for that'. I can look back and laugh at it now but at the time for the first ten seconds or so it was not funny one bit.

If it had been one of the other lads they might not have got away so easily but Dennis was great about it and looked after me a lot.

As did all my older and more experienced team-mates. I used to run past a lot of them and I think they thought 'we need to look after this kid, he might do well for us'.

Nigel Quashie also deserves a special mention as he was one of the main players who would always encourage me and look after me on the pitch. If anyone was kicking me a lot he would go after them and sort them out.

Despite losing to Leeds, ending our bizarre sequence of stalemates, there were still positives to take from the overall performance and Harry really believed we would go back up to the Premier League if we kept playing like that. I certainly went away feeling happy and confident.

I personally went on a bit of a run, scoring away at Millwall four days later in a 2-0 win and then again at home to Stoke the following week to help us win by the same scoreline.

When I get goals I always seem to go on a run and that continues up to this very day. Hitting the back of the net is a brilliant feeling. The emotion it creates is something hard to put into words.

All my early goals for Saints were very different, which showed my growing confidence to score from a variety of situations.

I quite liked the Millwall one where I judged the ball coming back from the defender and nipped round to score from an acute angle.

And then at home to Stoke it was a one-on-one with the goalkeeper which I put away comfortably in front of the Northam Stand.

The goals and success started to get my name noticed but I never really paid attention to anything other than the football.

I was still in the academy lodge sharing a room with Gareth Bale at the time. The staff there were very protective and made sure to keep us focused.

I continued to room with Gareth for a couple of years right up until I moved to Arsenal. We would just do what normal teenagers did like pop to the cinema, go bowling, play a few PlayStation games, nip to the sweet shop or watch films.

He was good company but you were always grateful if you got to your room unscathed when Gareth was around as he was a bit of a prankster, I had to be wary. He would do stunts like putting water on the top of your door to try and soak you as you walked in and silly things like that.

You always knew you were in trouble when you came back from a restaurant or visit away and the lights were turned off, something would happen.

But when you have so many young lads living together you will always have practical jokes happening. It never went too far though and nothing took our focus off training.

It was the family nature of the club and great academy set-up that, as an 11-year-old kid, made me decide to turn down Chelsea and head for the south coast.

Malcolm Elias, who scouted me from Swindon where I had been for six months, focussed on showing me the academy side of things.

I did have a look around Chelsea's Stamford Bridge but it was quite daunting because I actually went into the first team dressing room and for someone of my age I found it a little bit too much.

At Saints I was shown what they did to develop players and saw examples of some of the greats they had produced in the past. It felt right for me.

The main target I felt was to look at the home-grown players and not just look straight into the first team because you are miles and miles away from that.

As an 11-year-old you just want to play your football and enjoy it so Southampton seemed like the perfect place.

Another big plus point for me was they included my dad in the decision as well.

In the end it was without doubt the best decision I ever made. Time tells now when you look at the players they have developed to play at the top level.

They will continue to bring up the best players as well as it is an unbelievable club and one I am proud to have played for.

I know it would have been very difficult to do but I sometimes wonder what it might have been like if Southampton had been able to keep my team-mates from the youth side together.

Image how speedy a front four of myself, Gareth, Adam Lallana and Nathan Dyer would have been! We certainly would have given any defence a tough time.

I have such happy memories from playing in the academy squad that reached the Youth Cup Final. There was such a great atmosphere all the time between the players.

On the wings you had me and Nathan. We would always switch sides to try and make it hard for the full-backs, Adam was great to play with as well.

All of us had a good relationship on the pitch and a good bond off it, living together at the lodge where all the youth players used to live.

We had a great group that year. A lot of clubs always seem to have 'the next big thing' but at Southampton it always comes through. They always do it right.

I do not know the exact formula but I think it is because from an early age they get you enjoying playing football and have a great group of coaches.

We had England rugby World Cup winning coach Sir Clive Woodward around us at that point which I always enjoyed.

He would take some training methods from rugby and bring them to us and it did work until Martin Crainie picked up a hamstring injury and it all faded away.

Sir Clive is a very smart guy and was very interesting to be around. You instantly wanted to listen to him and hear what he had to say.

One day he brought all the academy guys around to his flat and explained everything in precise detail, what he wanted from us and his ideas for the club.

With the help of people like Clive and all the coaches and staff at the club I certainly matured and grew up as a person on and off the pitch.

In the December, I was shortlisted for the BBC Young Sports Personality of the Year. I didn't win but picked up the gong the following year.

It wasn't a shock when I left for Arsenal as I was aware if a big offer came in the club would find it hard to turn the money down.

But despite leaving after only a handful of games and goals I will never forget those early years as they were so important in my development.

I enjoy coming back to St Mary's as it brings back such great memories. I always try my best to thank the fans for what they did for me and it means a lot that I still have a good relationship with them.

They have been superb and I will always have a lot of respect for them. I want them to do well and they are the first result I look for after an Arsenal game.

It has been an enjoyable experience to reminisce about this part of my career. When Gareth and I roomed together we used to chat about what our futures could be like and how it would feel to score on our debuts.

I guess what we have both gone on to achieve shows schoolboy wishes can come true.

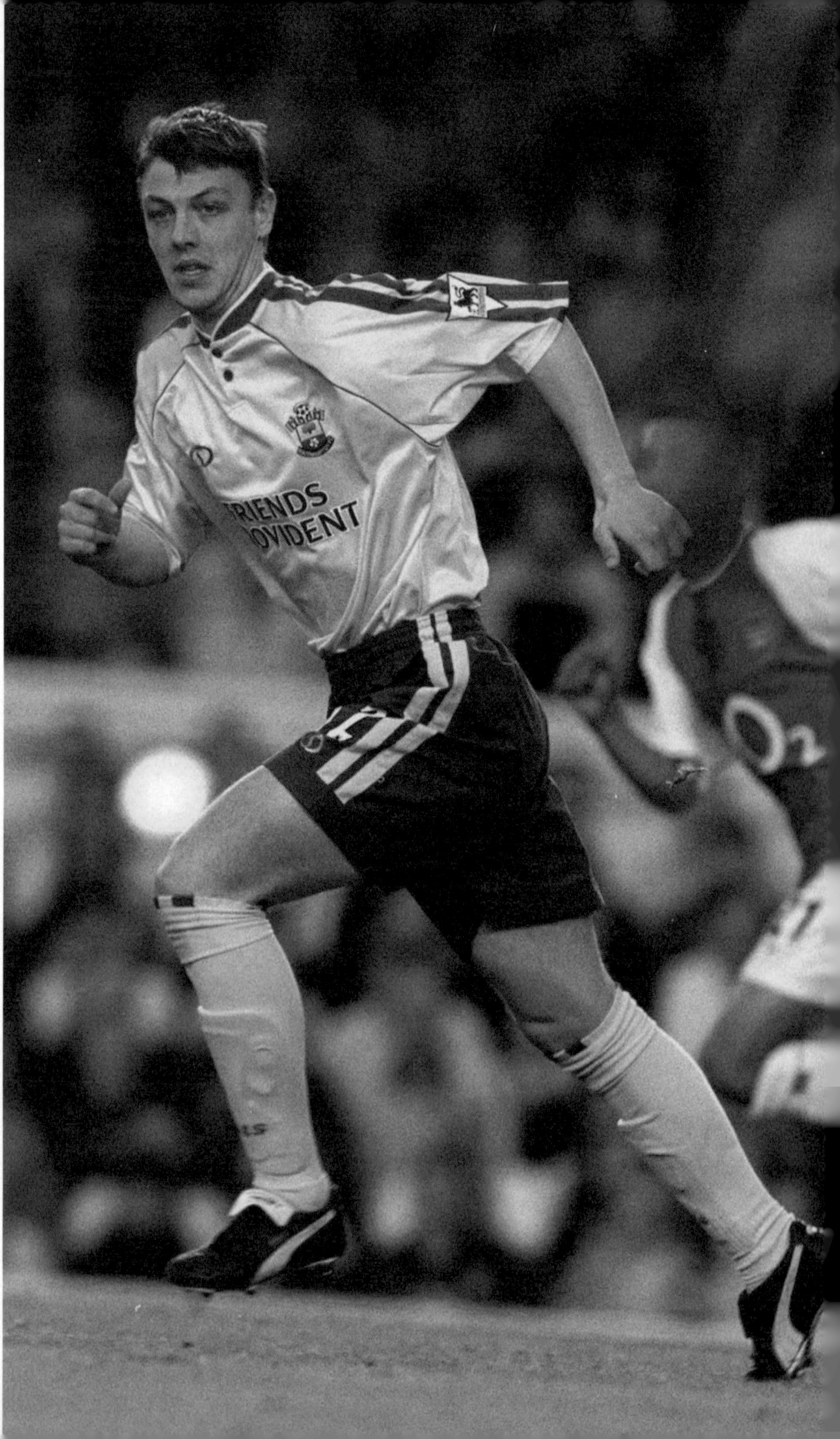

CHRIS BAIRD

Chris Baird

Arsenal 1 (Pires)

Southampton 0

FA Cup Final

Wembley, Saturday 17 May 2003

Southampton: Niemi (Jones 65), Bridge, Lundekvam, M Svensson, Baird (Fernandes, 87), Telfer, A Svensson (Tessem, 75), Oakley, Marsden, Ormerod, Beattie

IT STARTED like any normal reading out of the team line-up. 'Antti, you're in goal. Bridgey at left-back. Bairdy, you are on the right of the defence.' Now my ears had pricked up.

I kept thinking I must have misheard our manager Gordon Strachan. Surely he didn't just say my name in the starting XI for the FA Cup Final against Arsenal?

Politely, I let him finish because I didn't want to interrupt him as it was also a huge moment for all my fellow players.

But as soon as he had stopped I had to ask him again. I walked over to him in the room in our hotel in Cardiff and tapped him on the shoulder. 'Gaffer, am I actually playing?'

Gordon said yes and my jaw hit the floor, as did those of a few of my team-mates who were as stunned as I was.

Jason Dodd was injured at the time so I think that was a major part of the reason why I got the nod to play. I spoke to the gaffer in more detail and he explained how Paul Telfer would be in front of me.

Paul, being a stalwart of the game, really helped me and we spoke about how we would go about it.

There were a lot of experienced players in the team and people who had been playing all season. Some were incredibly disappointed as they didn't even make the squad or get on the bench.

Our French winger Fabrice Fernandes was one of the disappointed ones who had lost his place in the side. He did not say much to be honest and was very quiet although he didn't really say much any other time.

I know Fabrice would not have been happy but I have been in that situation before, when you think you should be playing and don't.

It is hard but, this may sound selfish, I wasn't too concerned, I was just delighted that I was playing. I am sure the other lads were glad for me as well in their own way but disappointed for the ones that weren't selected.

I was gobsmacked and over the moon to be involved in a game of that magnitude; it being the first FA Cup Final Saints had been involved in since 1976.

I still could not believe it myself that I was even in the squad, which had been named on the Wednesday, and was just so glad to be involved in this once in a lifetime fixture.

I was just 21-years-old and had only 158 minutes of first team football under my belt. I had not even been on the bench for any of the previous rounds. In fact, I had travelled up to Villa Park to watch the semi-final 2-1 win over Watford from the stands.

I was sat in my seat and when we won I was so pleased for the lads but a bit jealous as at that stage I still did not think I had any chance of making the bench for the final.

How wrong I was. My first experience of playing in the famous old competition would be walking out at the Millennium Stadium alongside an Arsenal team featuring some of the best players the Premier League has ever seen.

With all the history behind the FA Cup, it is tough to explain what I felt. People dream of playing in the final and fight for their whole career to try and achieve it and there's me just being thrown in at the deep end straight away.

It is one of my greatest achievements in football.

We travelled to Wales on the Thursday before the game, arrived and did a bit of training. It wasn't until the day before the match on the Friday that Gordon named the team.

The first thing I did was ring my girlfriend, who is now my wife, and she could not believe it. I then rang my parents and there would have been some celebrations I am sure!

None of them could work out if I was telling the truth or not. They were still getting over the shock of me being in the squad let alone the starting XI for one of the biggest games in the world.

I think a few of them were going to put a few bets on at the bookies to see who was going to be playing and I remember they were all chuffed to bits as they made a bit of spending money for the trip over.

They would have got some good odds on me starting that is for sure. No one had really heard of me until a few games beforehand so the bookies must have been thinking 'what, these boys are crazy'.

Our hotel was superb and everyone had their own rooms overlooking the river. I didn't mind being by myself but I am sure some players in my position wouldn't have minded a senior player reassuring them the night before.

When we woke up on match day, we saw Tim Lovejoy, the *Soccer Am* presenter, going past our windows on a boat with the match ball.

We had a great view over the water and somebody knocked on my door and said to have a look at the ball I would be following out of the tunnel just a few hours later.

Everyone was asking if I was nervous which was a fair question in the circumstances but I was not too bad and was very focused on what I had to do.

I had played against the Gunners nine days before and knew the kind of challenge that would be awaiting me and that helped with my nerves.

We got spanked 6-1 in the league in what was being touted as the dress rehearsal for the cup final. It was a real baptism of fire for me as I came on for Fabrice after 27 minutes when we were already 5-0 down!

It wasn't the best situation to be in but personally it was just nice to be on the Highbury pitch doing what I always wanted to do, play football.

I felt like I acquitted myself well after making my entrance on the big stage and like to claim a moral victory as we drew 1-1 during my time on the pitch.

But I am sure my display that day was not the only thing that got me my starting spot.

Firstly, I came on in midfield to play the holding role just to stop more goals coming in and to help the back four be a bit tighter.

I had a part in our goal as well when I played the ball in to Wayne Bridge who set up Jo Tessem for our solitary consolation.

Not that it counted for much as Robert Pires and Jermaine Pennant had already taken advantage of our off day to score a hat-trick each.

Little did I know at the time I would be crossing paths with the enigmatic Frenchman Pires soon after.

The heavy punishment we had taken did not leave any scars. The 1-0 win away at Manchester City the following week, my first ever Premier League start, in our final league match had put that to bed.

Being on the end of a 6-1 scoreline is never good but I think playing them again so soon, we definitely wanted some kind of revenge.

It wasn't to be on the day but we put in a much better performance and at least gave our supporters a huge amount of pride.

It was disappointing to lose but just to be playing in that stadium and to see the fans was incredible.

They were dressed in the yellow and blue away colours, the same as we wore in '76 and when they started singing and making a noise it was a phenomenal view.

I first took everything in when I was walking out of the tunnel. We were on the left hand side and that was where our fans were sitting and they went all the way around to the halfway line.

After that initial wall of yellow and blue I lost myself in the game and didn't really notice what was going on in the stands as I was so focused.

The stadium's retractable roof was shut though so made thinking difficult at times as the noise went up a few decibels and made the atmosphere all the more unbelievable. There was certainly no place for me to hide on the big pitch and I was right in the thick of the action from the whistle, as was my defensive partner Claus Lundekvam.

He could have been sent off inside 24 seconds for a tug on Thierry Henry, who had picked up a ball from Freddie Ljungberg down the right hand side.

Claus was last man but Henry didn't go down and used his pace to get away and force an early save from Antti Niemi.

Fair play to Graham Barber, the referee, as he played the advantage when, quite honestly, he could have stopped it and given Claus his marching orders for a deliberate pull.

If we had gone down to ten men so early on it would have been a nightmare but thankfully Antti rescued us.

Antti, who I went on to play with at Fulham, was superb and one of the greatest goalkeepers I have ever played with.

All eyes were on me in the eighth minute when Henry hit a shot which Niemi fumbled. The rebound fell to Dennis Bergkamp but I read the danger and got back to block his shot on the line.

It kept us in the game and we were still nervous at the time with it being so early on. It was very important for me to be in the right place at the right time. Trying to work out how to stop Bergkamp and Henry et al in their pomp was not an easy task.

That side were well on the way to becoming the 'invincibles' and went on to win the league the following season without losing a game.

We had a lot of fit players and a lot of legs in the team though such as our captain Chris Marsden and the experienced Telfer.

Chris, being at the end of his career, demonstrated infectious enthusiasm and seeing how excited he was made me even more determined to savour every moment. He had grafted all his career to be on this stage and we all wanted to put in a performance for our skipper.

We were setting up just trying to be compact and hard to beat and obviously try and do something with the ball as well and cause them a few problems.

Anders Svensson volleyed over the bar for our first opportunity on 15 minutes and we were growing into the game.

An impartial viewer might have been thinking it was becoming the Chris Baird show as moments later I had David Seaman, who was captaining them in the absence of the injured Patrick Vieira, sprawling to keep my shot out.

I won the ball in midfield, side-stepped past Henry, got away from Pires and curled a 25-yard shot for the bottom corner which Seaman, on his last appearance for Arsenal, kept out.

Unbelievable. A boy from Ballymoney in Northern Ireland with very little experience skipping away from a World Cup winner in Henry!

It was great for me not to be anonymous in the game. I was up against Pires for most of the afternoon so I was never going to be quiet.

We were confident but after James Beattie had a goal ruled out for offside the North Londoners took the lead with seven minutes remaining in the half.

Ray Parlour played it up to Henry, who sent Bergkamp down the right. The Dutchman crossed for Ljungberg but his shot was blocked by Claus.

With Michael Svensson and me scrambling to try and get the rebound, Pires nipped in to have one touch and rifle right-footed past our Finnish stopper Niemi.

I seem to remember throwing my arms down in disgust in the direction of Michael, who was on the floor, but it was not his fault and was just an emotional reaction to the goal.

We gave it a good go in the second half, Arsenal still dominated possession but we had chances to get the equaliser and force extra time.

The rock solid Seaman saved brilliantly from Brett Ormerod after 83 minutes when our little striker smashed a volley goalwards from a tight angle. Seeing the ball fly across the goal line and not into the net was heart-breaking as I thought it was heading in.

Then, in the fourth minute of injury time, we earned ourselves a corner. Matt Oakley whipped it in and James bundled two defenders out the way to get his head on the ball.

It was in all the way and I think the fans were just about to celebrate until Ashley Cole managed to clear it out for another corner. The next thing we knew it was the final whistle.

I watched that last bit of drama from the bench as I came off with three minutes to go with Fabrice getting on.

Gordon said to me straight away, with the fans on their feet giving me a standing ovation, I should be proud of myself and I'd had a fantastic game.

I sat down on the touchline in a daze. What had just happened? I was later named the Saints Man of the Match to round off a special day.

Our Scottish manager was fantastic and I do not have a bad word to say about him. He cared about his players, worked us hard and made sure we did everything properly. Nothing was left unturned. He would join in training now and again and he could still play let me tell you.

The knowledge he had gained being at Manchester United and Leeds, he brought all of that to us and helped us develop no end. We got a lot stronger and fitter and tried to play good football.

Despite the perception of him being uptight and fiery, Gordon was very calm and collected in the changing room beforehand.

I was concentrating on what I had to do. More often than not before a game of this magnitude everyone will be quite calm and just telling each other to go out and enjoy it and leave nothing out on the pitch.

For us, getting to the final was special but for defending champions Arsenal, after thrashing us 6-1 and having experience in finals, they probably thought they would win easily.

It was completely different for us, a one-off game of football and we were going to give everything we had.

We got the runners-up medals and went over to our section of fans to thank them for their support. I still have the medal in the box on show at my house.

Sometimes I think it could have been a winners' medal but then I think 'hang on', I was just happy to be involved.

For only my second ever start to be in that game I still enjoy looking back on it now and it is still overwhelming.

Afterwards, even though we lost we made the most of it. We had a little party with a few drinks with family and friends.

I had got tickets for everyone, parents, brothers, sisters, girlfriends. I think I had nine or ten tickets for them which were gratefully received.

For us it was just a chance to talk about our achievement of getting to the final and for me, to think about how far I had come in a short space of time.

Before my debut against Aston Villa, just two months prior to the final, the highlight of my career had been reserve team football. I had only been on the bench for the first team a handful of times.

Obviously, playing with the reserves is a lot different and when you are training with the first team, which I was really enjoying, you want to be joining them on a Saturday.

When I replaced David Prutton in that 2-2 draw at Villa Park I felt ready to contribute to the side but my next appearance, as I have said, was not one to remember with the routing by Arsenal.

As I was so new to the squad I didn't have any particularly close pals as most of them were a lot older than me.

I got on well with all of them but mainly kept myself to myself, showed them respect and kept my head down.

Wayne Bridge, who occupied the left flank and was a marvellous talent, was a couple of years older than me so I would speak to him more than the rest.

Everyone was great to me and gave me a lot of support. It was a fantastic group and we were 100 per cent together, a proper team.

Unfortunately for the following two seasons after my meteoric rise I struggled to be a part of that amazing team again.

I went back to Southampton after the game and that is when it hit me. I went on holiday and tried to quickly get back to normality, but it was difficult. I think maybe people thought I came back the following season thinking I had made it. I could have done a bit more and the situation with the managers didn't help either

It didn't quite happen for me. Gordon left me out and then left his post, while Paul Sturrock, Steve Wigley and Harry Redknapp had different ideas on me through what was a turbulent time for the club.

I could probably have done a bit more in training and improved my attitude, not that it was bad, but I just could not get a game.

The next two seasons I played only a handful of times. I got sent out on loan to Watford and Walsall which brought me back down to earth but I absolutely loved my time at both clubs as I was playing football, which was the most important thing.

I didn't properly cement my place until the 2006/07 season under George Burley in the Championship, playing centre-half.

I got player of the season, goal of the season and won loads of awards which was nice. I was playing, enjoying myself, full of confidence and happy.

Just like I was when I came over as a 16-year-old straight out of school from Northern Ireland to start my scholarship.

The academy is phenomenal and I was very lucky to be a part of it. All I ever wanted to do was play football, I was always going to give it a go and hope I was good enough, which thankfully I was with great help from the top coaches at the club.

Even up until now they are still bringing the players through and I should know, I have had to try and stop some of them on a Saturday!

With the likes of Theo Walcott, Gareth Bale, Adam Lallana, Nathan Dyer and Alex Oxlade-Chamberlain alongside all the others, the list is endless.

After my surprise selection in the cup final I think some of the younger lads would have looked up to me at the time and thought, wow, if he can do it then so can I.

That is a strange thought, Gareth Bale looking up to me! In his long list of achievements and trophies, he hasn't got an FA Cup runners-up medal yet, which shows how prestigious it is and lucky I am.

As a youngster I was a big Manchester United fan so would watch the finals on TV and dream of getting there one day.

Some great players never get the chance and I always like to remind my team-mates I have played in one. As it was so long ago and no one had heard of me they don't even realise I did it.

Everywhere I have gone I have tried to do my best and get to the final of the competition again but at least I have the memory of doing it once.

The FA Cup still stands out for me more than the gruelling 2-1 Europa League Final defeat to Atletico Madrid while at Fulham in 2010.

In fact, the only game that might run it close is a certain 1-0 win over England in Belfast in 2005.

It is still surreal to think my best memory of the FA Cup is my first memory. I would like to put on record my thanks to Gordon for giving me a day my family and I will never forget. It took great courage on his part.

I think I am the only person to ever make their debut in the FA Cup in the final of the competition and it will make a great quiz question one day.

One that, no doubt, only Saints fans who joined me on that magical day at the Millennium Stadium will be able to answer.

CLAUS LUNDEKVAM

Claus Lundekvam

Southampton 3 (Kachloul 2, Le Tissier)

Arsenal 2 (Cole, Ljungberg)

Premier League
The Dell, Saturday 19 May 2001

Southampton: P Jones, Monk (El Khalej, 74), Lundekvam, Richards, Bridge, Kachloul (Benali, 81), Tessem, Marsden, Pahars, Davies (Le Tissier, 74), Beattie

IT IS not unusual at the end of a successful season for players to perform a lap of honour around the pitch to thank the fans for their support, but this was no usual lap of honour and no ordinary season.

As I wandered around in a semi-daze attempting to peer through my own tears to survey the scene I could see grown men crying in the stands. This, after all, was the end of an era.

The time had come to say goodbye to a dear old friend, one that had been worth many precious points to the club through the decades.

I am not talking about a much-loved team-mate. I am talking about The Dell. The place I still regard as home even after all these years since the bulldozers moved in.

By the time we played host to Arsenal on the last day of the season neither side had much to play for, on the face of it at least.

We were comfortable in mid-table and they were already guaranteed runners-up spot, a distant second behind Manchester United who had long since been crowned Premier League champions.

But for us Saints players the match was very special because we knew it was the last time we would ever play a competitive fixture at the ground we all loved so much.

It was a great moment for the whole city, supporters, players and everybody involved with the club.

My memory of the game is blurred but I can still picture the winning goal, scored by 'Mr Southampton' himself Matt Le Tissier, as if it were yesterday.

The whole thing was like a fairytale and it felt like it was just meant to happen; for Matt to come on as substitute and conjure up one more magic moment on a ground where he had given our supporters so many wonderful memories.

We were all stunned and it was a fantastic moment because it was such a cracking strike.

Our goalkeeper Paul Jones punted the ball long upfield and it was flicked into the box by James Beattie. What happened next was the perfect end to 103 years at The Dell.

Matt took the ball down with his right foot just inside the penalty area and swivelled his body before bending the most sweetly-struck left-foot volley into the top corner past a helpless Alex Manninger.

Looking back at video replays of the goal, which I have seen hundreds of times over down the years, I sprinted as fast as I could to run the length of the pitch so I could join the rest of my team-mates in mobbing Matt.

I was just ecstatic and there was so much joy and happiness on the faces of everyone around me.

It was one of the most treasured moments of my playing career for so many reasons. You bond with certain players and Matt was one of those I struck it off with straight away.

He was such a good player that we all looked up to him, but he was so down to earth and looked after me from day one.

He always made sure I was all right and when he split up from his wife we spent a lot of time together. We hung out quite a lot at that time and he stayed with me in my townhouse at Ocean Village for a while when my wife was back in Norway.

He later bought the house from me and then sold it to Shane Warne, the world-famous Australian cricketer when he was playing for Hampshire, so that place has seen some memories.

One day when Matt was staying over we had a little bet on the game that if we won and he scored I would give him a case of Malibu and Coke, which I turned up with a few days after the match.

It set me back a few quid to fulfil my promise to him but it was well worth it because I had an agreement with the club who would give me a bonus if we finished in the top ten in the table and those three points secured our place in the top half.

Malibu and Coke was always Matt's drink of choice on our team nights out because he never drank pints and got a lot of abuse for that from the rest of the players because we used to tell him it was a ladies' drink.

We always prepared for our home games in the same way and the routine for this game was no different to any other despite the enormity of the occasion.

We met up at the Southampton Park Hotel for lunch and drove down to the ground a couple of hours before kick-off, soaking up the carnival atmosphere as the coach weaved through the streets on the way to the ground.

Leading up to it the whole city was talking about this last game and I think the emotion that was swirling around among the supporters helped us win the game.

That coupled with the fact we had the chance to finish in the top half meant we wanted it more than Arsenal, who were still getting over losing a dramatic FA Cup Final to a Michael Owen-inspired Liverpool the previous weekend.

As I have already said my memory of the rest of the 90-plus minutes is not the best but looking back at the record books I now know Arsenal led twice and we turned it around twice before winning it a minute from time thanks to my mate Matt.

I remember Beattie had missed a good early chance before Ashley Cole put Arsenal in front in the 28th minute, lashing the ball home at the second time of asking after Jones has saved his initial shot.

We were given a bit of a helping hand for our equaliser early in the second half when Arsenal's French defender Gilles Grimandi drilled a clearance into Chris Marsden and the ball broke kindly for Hassan Kachloul to chip it into the net.

Freddie Ljungberg restored Arsenal's lead, rounding off a trademark counter attacking move from the Gunners only for Kachloul to equalise for a second time from close range after Manninger had flapped at a cross from our young full-back Garry Monk.

Hassan was a bit of a character, with a French-Moroccan style and always had a joke to tell. He always wanted to impress in the fashion stakes and whenever we went out on the town he was sure to be wearing a flashy outfit.

Hassan was a good player too who would go on to play for Aston Villa and Wolverhampton Wanderers after leaving us.

We may not have got our storybook ending had a cracking strike from Patrick Vieira not been kept out by a post but it seems poetic justice Le Tissier had the last word.

My centre-back partner that day was Dean Richards. He was a fantastic player and such a nice guy who passed away too early.

I remember Glenn Hoddle, our former manager, taking Deano to Spurs and I would like to claim some credit for that move because I partnered him from the minute he came to the club.

He was a great defender and, but for his injuries would have gone on to win many England caps. I have very fond memories of Dean and his family. It was an honour when I was asked to take part in a pre-match memorial for him when we played Wolves at Molineux after his death, which shocked me deeply.

Wayne Bridge, who played at left-back, may not have been the sharpest tool in the box but was another top player and someone I bonded with for many years.

I still speak to him and even after he went to Chelsea and became an international star with England we had nights out in London.

I still keep in contact with so many of that team, which may be unusual but that says all you need to know about the spirit we had in the camp.

I got on particularly well with Marian Pahars and Beattie, who both went into management after they had hung up their shooting boots.

I have to say if there was one guy I never saw as a manager it was Beattie because he was such a Jack the lad character with his flash suits and big ties. The fact we had to beat a team of the quality of Arsenal to give The Dell a winning send-off also adds to the magic.

Their front two that day were Thierry Henry and Dennis Bergkamp, two of the best strikers the Premier League has ever seen and I always loved testing myself against opponents of that stature.

They also had people like Martin Keown, Tony Adams and Cole at the back, Robert Pires and Ljungberg weaving their spell in midfield and then there was Vieira, a formidable competitor and leader in the middle of the park.

That Arsene Wenger sent out such a strong line-up showed the respect he had for our team and we would go on to face many of the same players when Arsenal beat us 1-0 in the FA Cup Final a couple of years later.

For most players appearing in the cup final would be the most memorable match of their life but for raw emotion the last game at The Dell edges it for me.

In those days there was quite a big drinking culture at the club and we hit the town for about four nights straight after the game. I could not and did not sleep for days because I had so much adrenaline flowing around my body.

The whole city was overjoyed about the result, finishing in the top ten and a great season. We were treated very well in whatever bar or nightclub we whiled away the hours in.

I do not think anyone begrudged us our partying after nine intense months building up to the final curtain call. We all knew when we kicked our first ball in anger the previous August this would be the last season at The Dell and wanted to have a good campaign, to finish on a high and leave with good memories.

I have to confess that when I first signed for Southampton I had never heard of The Dell. I did not even speak any English.

It was the autumn of 1996 and there were only a few Norwegians playing in the Premier League at the time but there was a boom a few years later.

By the time I retired there were about 20 of us, which was quite amazing.

I was bought by Graeme Souness, who came to watch me twice playing for SK Brann in my homeland along with big Lawrie McMenemy, the most successful manager in Saints' history and at the time the club's director of football.

After the second game we had a meeting and I signed for Southampton that night so clearly they liked what they saw. Obviously they had done their research beforehand and sent some scouts over to watch me.

It was an exciting moment for me because like most Scandinavians I had grown up watching English football, the FA Cup Final and knew a bit about the history of the game in this country but did not know anything about Saints as a club or even where the city was on a map.

In those days the Internet was not as prevalent as it is now so it was very much a step into the unknown for me.

Within a week of signing the contract I had flown over to begin my new life in the UK and within ten days I played my first game; a 2-2 draw with Nottingham Forest at The Dell.

The first time I saw the stadium the word that sprung to mind was cosy. It was very intense and intimidating because the crowd were right on top of you. It was a tight ground with tiny facilities.

But for me everything was brand new and exciting.

I remember being very nervous and thinking 'oh my God, this is proper football' because of the physical side of it and the intensity of the game. It was so frantic it was unbelievable. It was a shock to the body and to the head.

The noise was deafening and the loudness of the crowd and the tempo of the game were a world apart from what I had been used to in Scandinavia.

I don't remember much about my debut because I was so nervous and had only been training with the boys for two or three days before playing. I had not had much time to think.

I was very young and naïve and thought I could play my style of football, which was very laid back and I liked to contribute going forward by stepping out of defence and play from the back and go on my little mazy runs.

Souness had even compared me to the great Liverpool legend Alan Hansen because of the way I played but I quickly found out you did not get as much chance to show off your footballing skills as a Premier League defender.

My second game was away to Liverpool at Anfield, whom I supported as a kid because my grandmother was born there, so that was a special moment.

I remember walking down the steps in the tunnel and I reached up and touched the famous 'This is Anfield' sign as I had seen the Liverpool players do so many times on TV. Our kit man, Malcolm 'Woggy' Taylor, was behind me and he said 'What the hell are you doing Claus?' I think I got a bit swept up in the moment.

I only ever scored two goals for Southampton, one away at Wolves and the other at home to Cardiff at St Mary's, so sadly I never managed to net at The Dell.

I used to have to endure a lot of stick from my team-mates about that because I was absolutely useless in front of goal in proper games.

In training I was pretty good but in matches it was a mental thing. I would stick my head in and break my neck in my own box to defend a goal but in the opposition penalty area I simply did not do that.

Gordon Strachan, one of my many Saints managers, also passed on a few comments on my lack of goals to the media but that did not overly bother me because it was not my job. As a midfielder or a striker you are expected to contribute to scoring but in my position I was happy to try and keep them out of our net.

The Dell was always special for me. I saw it as a safe place and as players we felt it gave us an advantage because if we were on our game you could sense the fear of the away side.

The crowd were always awesome for us and every away team hated coming down.

They knew it was a tight pitch with the fans close to the action and they always met a Saints side that was in their faces straight from the first whistle.

Opponents never took us lightly at The Dell because we were always very aggressive early on, that was our way and we had a fantastic team spirit. During the first four or five seasons I was there we stayed up purely because of that spirit. We went out there willing to die for each other and the dressing room was very strong.

We bonded straight away and I remember Jason Dodd, Francis Benali, Le Tissier, Ken Monkou, Jim Magilton and Neil Maddison were all leaders. I can still remember all their voices booming around our cramped dressing room.

Benali was very professional, very strict. He was the nicest guy ever off the pitch but as soon as he got on the training field or crossed the white line for a match he turned into a monster. It was quite frightening sometimes.

He was so passionate on the pitch and you could see the anger boiling up inside before he started throwing himself into tackles.

Magilton was always the centre of attention on our nights out because after two pints he could not see anything. He was such a lightweight.

Those early years taught me if you have a strong dressing room it can take you a long way. We knew we didn't have the best team on paper at all but we had some special players like Le Tissier who we could depend on to score goals.

But our unit and togetherness was our strength.

We were always together off the pitch and if you build relations away from the training ground you can take that onto the field with you. You get something special from not wanting to let your team mates down.

From the first day I arrived I was involved with the English boys, going out socialising and that was probably my strength; being able to join them as a foreign player and becoming part of the team as quickly as possible.

I loved the English culture, the way of living and everything about it.

Everything about The Dell was unique compared to places like Anfield and Old Trafford.

The tunnel was tight, the corridors were so narrow and the little warm-up area we used to use on matchdays was very old-school.

It was an old ground with everything made of wood, including the benches in the changing rooms but all our players felt at home there because it was ours.

I remember driving to home games feeling very nervous but as soon as I pulled up in the car park I would think 'This is my home' and that enabled me to lower my shoulders and say, 'This is what I do, this is what I love.'

I loved the intimidating feeling of playing against the best strikers every week.

I was very excited when we were told we would be moving from The Dell to a new £30m stadium and we all felt it was about time.

In order to stay in the Premier League we had to move to a bigger ground with better facilities. We all understood it needed to happen but leaving The Dell was pretty emotional.

After the Arsenal game, which goes down in the record books as the last official game there, our south coast neighbours Brighton came down to play a friendly as they had been the club's first ever opponents at the stadium back in 1898.

That too was a very sad occasion because we knew we were saying goodbye to so much history.

After the final whistle was blown for the last time we went back into the tunnel for a couple of minutes and then came back out and did a lap of honour with the fans still crammed inside.

The dressing room was a very subdued place and everyone sat there in silence, realising we had come to the end of the line.

All the boys I mentioned like Le Tissier and Franny Benali who had been with the club all their lives, were visibily affected by the finality of the situation, which was a natural feeling to have.

I stayed in Southampton for a few years after I retired from playing and whenever I drove past The Dell the memories came flooding back, with the little pub on the corner and everything around the area is connected with the ground, like apartment blocks named after former players.

I have lost count of the number of times we were playing at St Mary's and I drove to The Dell by mistake, taking the wrong turn at the roundabout at the top of The Avenue.

When you move to a new ground it takes some time to get used to that. It is like playing away and we struggled a bit in the first few months at St Mary's because we had lost that feeling of having the comfort of your own environment.

In fact our form was so bad to begin with the club even went to the extreme lengths of getting a witch doctor in to bless the pitch because they thought it was cursed, but I did not believe in that.

I have never been one to show my emotions but am not too macho to admit I have shed many a tear over leaving The Dell.

Just playing the video of Matt's goal still chokes me up but my memories of that special place will stay in my heart forever and I am grateful I have been given the chance to put down in writing what the place meant to me.

MARIAN PAHARS

Marian Pahars

Southampton 2 (Pahars 2)

Everton 0

Premier League
The Dell, Sunday 16 May 1999

Southampton: Jones, Dodd, Monkou, Lundekvam, Benali, Marsden, Kachloul, Le Tissier (Ostenstad, 85), Hughes, Pahars (Beresford, 80), Beattie

IT MAY sound strange seeing as I had just scored the goals to keep Southampton in the Premier League, but I had very little idea of the importance of my contribution as I battled my way off the pitch through throngs of our delirious supporters.

All I could think about was how differently things could have turned out for me.

I had my work permit rejected three times before I finally got the all-clear to travel over to England and start my career at Southampton.

While waiting for it all to be sorted I had a few agonising weeks at home and during that time an offer came from Salernitana, who were then playing in the top division in Italy, Serie A.

It was a good offer and the owners of the club talked to me and asked whether it was maybe not worth waiting for Southampton.

For me it was not a big issue whether I was going to Italy, Spain or England because in Latvia we all dream of playing in any of these big European leagues.

I could easily have gone to Salernitana, but in the end I told them 'no chance'. While I still had hope of getting the correct paperwork I didn't want to join anybody but Saints.

They were the first team to offer me a chance and I did not forget that. I had been to look around the club and seen what it was like, I even watched a game to get a sense of the atmosphere and what the country was like.

It was the only place for me and I am so glad I stuck to my guns as I spent eight happy years there.

It was Gary Johnson, who has managed clubs like Yeovil Town and Bristol City in England, who helped make it all happen.

I was playing for my hometown team Skonto Riga and had a couple of good seasons in the first team, scoring plenty of goals and winning trophies.

I played against European giants Barcelona and Inter Milan in the Champions League qualifying stages when a scout saw me play against Inter and got in contact with Gary.

Gary, who later became the manager of the Latvian national team, came to Moscow to cast his eye over me soon after when I was playing in the Commonwealth tournament.

He must have liked what he saw as he called Dave Jones straight away to say I was decent. Dave duly invited me over for a trial and I was off and running.

Unfortunately I didn't work too much with Dave as he parted company with Saints soon after I signed but will remain one of the best coaches I had.

He believed in me, that is the most important thing. A couple of other people tried to offer me to some other clubs in England before Saints but it wasn't successful. Some managers liked me and some did not.

Dave gave me a chance and I am always grateful for that, I will always remember him. It was a shame he had to leave early.

In the trial I played for the reserves against Oxford United and scored a perfect hat-trick, one with my right foot, left foot and head.

Immediately after the game Saints got me to sign a contract. It was very easy to decide what to do despite me speaking no English whatsoever.

With the language issues the first few months were very difficult and confusing. I didn't speak a word and it was tough. For the first few months especially it was depressing. What made it worse was that I did not play as I came with an injury I had picked up from the national team.

I was without a home and stayed in a hotel with my pregnant wife so it was a difficult time and we were very lonely.

You go in the morning to training and sit on your own in the changing room. People came and attempted to talk but realised quickly it was impossible to communicate with me.

So you have to sit by yourself, watching everyone around you laughing and joking. It is not a nice feeling but makes you more determined to learn the language and perform on the pitch to gain your team-mates' respect.

I always remember the time I went back to the hotel where my wife was waiting for me and I was so down I said I did not want to go to training the next day. I just did not feel good inside.

I wanted to go straight to the airport and jump on the first flight home but she said to me I was crazy. She pointed out this was my chance to go and better myself and make my country and family proud.

The feeling came and went quickly but I still found it tough in the new country.

It was certainly nothing to do with the pressure of the transfer fee as I think some people might have been saying.

I was aware it was £800,000, which at the time was a lot of money for an unknown player but it did not affect me.

Despite not being able to talk to my team-mates off the field, on the pitch the language of football is universal and you understand with your senses what everyone is doing around you.

To be honest, in my mind I was playing better when I could not speak English because you don't need to talk much, you just feel when you are going to get a pass and where to run.

In results terms though my debut was a disaster, we lost against Coventry City who, like us, were one of the clubs threatened with relegation. People were writing us off, saying we could not get out of trouble now.

But as soon as I scored my first goal everything became better for me. The fans started to recognise me, the players who I played with started to come and speak to me and slowly I started to settle.

The release of pure relief and emotion when the ball hit the back of the net to grab the crucial equaliser in the 3-3 draw against Blackburn Rovers was special for me. I felt I had finally arrived.

Things started to go smoother. I have always thought if you do your job, people appreciate that. My job was to score goals.

I had to do that quickly as Southampton were in the thick of a grim battle for survival and had not been out of the bottom three all season by the time I was fit and ready to take the field.

Having said that, I did not know too much about the situation with the league table as I was just concentrating on my game and what I could do.

I certainly was not aware quite how important the Everton game was for the fans, club and area. If I had known I would have been a lot more nervous and maybe not played as well.

The first sign it was not just going to be a normal game was after the 2-0 win away at Wimbledon the week before.

We had a meeting with the fans in a pub somewhere on the way home. It was interesting and my first time ever doing something like that. Supporters came and talked to the players and I could not understand why we were there.

Now I realise, we had one game left to clinch survival and they wanted to say to us 'come on boys, you have to give it your all'.

I thought it was just a regular thing and it often happened after away games in England, I was very confused.

Dave Jones probably gave a rousing speech in the dressing room with senior players like Francis Benali, Jason Dodd and Matt Le Tissier all chipping in but it would have all gone over my head.

I will always be thankful to Franny as he was the one at the start who really tried to help me and get me settled.

I was from a small country and was not a famous player but he invited me to his home with my wife and helped me with everything.

Matt was the biggest hero at the club and I had seen some of his magical goals on TV before I arrived.

He was at the end of his career when I was there but you could see he had obvious talent and the skills to express himself.

He was never fully fit but would come on for 30 minutes to change the game. He did not need to run too much to make an impact. He was fantastic. If we were losing he would come on and alter events so we won.

He was a massive star and to watch him do little tricks in training was a joy to see. He was also a good member of the dressing room.

As was James Beattie, our recently voted player of the season, who had scored in the previous two crucial wins against Leicester and Wimbledon.

Beatts, as he was affectionately known, was an infectious personality and always very friendly, which helped us have a good partnership up front.

We didn't see each other much after the games but during training we spent a lot of time together working on things. I knew he was someone who would back me up on the pitch at any time.

Beatts was very strong physically and I never saw any defender who was going to beat him in the air under pressure, never.

I knew 100 per cent if the ball was in between the two defenders he was going to win it so with a bit of thinking and movement I could latch onto the flick-on. At that time we played a lot of football in the air rather than on the ground, it was a direct game and having his aerial advantage made it easy for me to play off him.

Despite only playing together a handful of times it was our quickly developing partnership that would keep us up on that tense final day.

He made so many goals for me and I made so many for him. As a striker you want to score goals, it is a great feeling but also I enjoyed it when I gave an assist. Neither of us were ever selfish.

Things we had worked on together in training happened in this game. The first goal on 25 minutes was a simple big-man small-man combination.

Jason Dodd launched a long ball forward and Beatts got up above the two big centre-backs, Dave Weir and Craig Short, to nod the ball into the open space. I was unmarked and made sure not to rush before placing the ball under Thomas Myhre from 15 yards.

I could almost hear the uncertainty and suspense from the spectators as they must have thought I took an eternity to tuck the ball away and open the scoring but I had to make sure.

The Dell erupted with the fans chanting really loudly, I later realised they were singing 'we are staying up'.

I loved The Dell and played the best matches of my football career there. It was a special place, no doubt.

Even now if you ask me I would say I would prefer to play at The Dell rather than St Mary's because the feel was different, a typical and historic English atmosphere.

You cannot recreate that with the new stadium unfortunately. When you used to come to The Dell, no other ground in the world was like it. It cannot be mixed with anything.

Many teams were afraid to play there and it is true, the fans could touch you and that is frightening. It was a good atmosphere and we fancied ourselves against anyone at that ground.

The place was rocking and Matt, who was outstanding on the day and seemed to relish the occasion, was very pumped up and almost got sent off for swearing at the referee in the first half.

Scoring any goal is incredible but this one felt a really big strike and it settled everyone down although Everton probably should have equalised soon after through Francis Jeffers.

Their young striker was played through one-on-one with our goalkeeper Paul Jones but his shot drifted agonisingly wide. It is moments like that when you start to believe it will be your day.

Our confidence was up and our attacking play started to improve with Matt nearly adding a second with a rasping 25-yard drive in first-half stoppage time.

Everton had nothing to play for and we were so much hungrier than them for the whole 90 minutes, but it took until the 68th minute for me to make the points safe with my third goal in six games.

Chris Marsden, another fine professional, dispossessed Olivier Dacourt and passed down the wing to Beatts, who got the better of two defenders and delivered a fantastic cross into the box.

I should never have won any headers being only 5ft 6in tall and with the likes of Weir, Short, David Unsworth and Dave Watson towering above me in their defence but I managed to stoop low and head past Myhre at the near post.

It was a challenge up against the big central defenders but I did not really care. Some of the best players in the world like Lionel Messi are just as small as me so it does not really matter.

The biggest issue is the speed of movement and thinking. I was quick on my feet and in my mind so that was my advantage.

When the ball hits the back of the net it is the best feeling in the world and you lose yourself for a few moments. It was a dream come true to score again.

Nottingham Forest and Blackburn were already down so we were competing with Charlton, who were at home to Sheffield Wednesday, for the dreaded last relegation place.

If we had lost and Charlton had won, we would have gone down, but we were not aware of their result on the pitch.

There did seem to be a party atmosphere in the stands though. Maybe some fans had radios on them and knew they were on their way to losing 1-0.

My last ten minutes on the pitch, before being substituted for John Beresford on 80 minutes, were magical and I so wanted a hat-trick.

It was not to be and I walked off to take my place in the dugout to a standing ovation from the supporters that left my spine tingling.

I hugged the manager who was relieved and it was nice for him to say of me after the game to the media, 'he is probably a bit better than what we thought'.

The press wanted to speak to me afterwards but they would have not got very far, so instead I joined in with the big lap of honour around the pitch to celebrate with the fans, who had been through so much anxiety over the course of the season.

When we finally made it back to the dressing room I wouldn't say the atmosphere was like after winning a trophy or anything – more just a feeling of relief we had stayed up.

I was then taken by club officials to some of the sponsors' lounges where they presented the man of the match awards.

I didn't understand what I was doing there but went with it as I was too tired to argue. In all the areas we went the fans were mad with happiness.

I remember a big lounge, I came in and everyone was buzzing like I had scored another goal and only then did I realise something big and important had happened.

My relationship with the paying public was very important to me and at the time I was not sure why they picked me as a favourite over many other good players.

Maybe it was because in all my time on the pitch, scoring or not, I was giving my all, absolutely everything.

Even when sometimes I didn't have anything left in the tank I still gave it a go and that is why I had the injuries as I never rested or shirked a tackle.

From the first day when I heard them singing or supporting me it helped me. Especially with my humble background, it meant so much to me and more than maybe anyone else.

We ended up five points ahead of the relegation zone, which looking back was incredible considering we only climbed out of the bottom three in the final week of the season.

It was a proper great escape and I was told we had preserved our 22nd consecutive year in the top division.

After the game I think some of my team-mates went out into the town and celebrated. I certainly did not and went straight back home to my family.

I had a good relationship with everyone but pubs and clubs were not for me. I was so out of the loop I did not even know players sometimes went out after games.

Maybe some of the squad would say I was never that social as I never went out with them but I was just a little bit shy.

I was still on a high on the pitch by the time the next season started and managed to score eight goals in my first 14 games.

My compatriot Imants Bleidelis also came over to join me which was great for me but sadly it did not work out for him.

Amazingly, the exact day he arrived at the training ground was the day Dave Jones left, you could not make it up.

He was Dave's signing and when Glenn Hoddle came he just did not need him, that was why he was never able to show his talent and I felt sorry for him as he was a really good player.

It was definitely nice to have him around though and was important for me, although I never thought he had been signed just to keep me company.

I enjoyed working with Glenn and we played really good football. It was one of my best seasons at the club with me finishing top scorer with 13 goals.

Everyone did their jobs well and we played against big teams in a strong league with no real fear of going down. I was loving it.

I even repeated the feat of scoring on the last day of the season against Wimbledon, which relegated them unfortunately.

Glenn left us for Tottenham the next campaign which was a blow but I had so many different managers in my time at the club I lost count.

In the end I would have liked to have stayed for ten years and maybe have a testimonial game, that was my only disappointment from my time at Saints.

That would have been special to top off my career but unfortunately the manager at the time, George Burley, had a different opinion. He didn't sell me, he just didn't renew my contract.

I don't think I ever really had a chance to say goodbye to the supporters and that is what hurts; hopefully I will get my chance one day.

It was very upsetting. At that time you think you give everything for so many years and then someone comes in for a couple of months and gets rid of you. But Burley had power at that time and was making decisions. I am not blaming him, I have had time to think about it. He was the manager and was just doing his job.

Maybe I was not at my best due to injuries but I had a lot of emotions and was very upset at the time. Now I look back and just think 'this is life'.

Southampton is, and will always be, my second home. My child was born there and I felt really settled in the later years. I have good friends there and have good feelings whenever I come back.

I do hope I will get a chance to return to the club in some capacity in the future, it would be special to go back as a manager.

I definitely have a connection to the club and like to see them doing well with the good young players.

There is nothing I would change looking back on it and reminding myself of that game against Everton has brought back nothing but good memories.

It kick-started my career in England with a lot of people really sitting up and taking note of me. I used to get called the 'Latvian Michael Owen' after that performance and I took it as a compliment.

The nickname stuck throughout my time at the club, I guess we both suffered with many injuries!

My goals on the south coast made me a national star back home in Latvia. Without my Southampton career that would probably never have happened.

I was the first Latvian to really succeed in the Premier League. I took my form for Saints back home to the national team and won the Player of the Year three years in a row until I got injured.

It was not just back home though, I made a name for myself in Europe also. People recognise me when I am on my travels and that is down to when I was poaching goals in the best league in the world.

Whatever it took, I had to take my chance at the big time and the script for my first few games at the end of that first season could not have been written better.

I would like to thank everyone at the club for helping me, especially the fans, sorry I never had a chance to say goodbye but let's hope I can say 'hello' again in the near future.

EGIL OSTENSTAD

Egil Ostenstad

Southampton 6
(Ostenstad 2, Le Tissier, Berkovic 2, Neville OG)

Manchester United 3 (Beckham, May, Scholes)

Premier League
The Dell, Saturday 26 October 1996

Southampton: Beasant, Dodd, Lundekvam, Neilson (Magilton, 75), van Gobbel, Dryden, Charlton (Potter, 70), Oakley, Berkovic, Le Tissier (Watson, 88), Ostenstad

WHEN MOST people think of Manchester United in the 1990s they remember Eric Cantona and his upturned collar or Ryan Giggs flying past defenders, but I recall the treble that never was and downing pints of Newcastle Brown Ale to celebrate one of the most famous victories in Saints' history.

Even if the record books say something else I still have the match ball in my house, so in my view I scored a hat-trick.

The fact United defender Gary Neville's was the last boot to touch the ball as my third goal rolled over the line is irrelevant to me. If it was an own goal there have been a lot of own goals in the history of football wrongly awarded.

This game was right at the beginning of my career at Southampton as I had only joined the club a month earlier after impressing the scouts playing for Viking Stavanger in my native Norway.

It was just my third game in the Premier League, my second start and I had not previously been able to get my name on the score-sheet.

To be involved in a match like this so early in my stint in England was a great start for me. It proved to myself I was good enough to play in the Premier League against the very best opponents, which United were.

Coming from the Norwegian league was a big step up and United, whom Sir Alex Ferguson had expertly guided to the league and FA Cup double a season earlier, were the biggest club in the country.

They were also the favourite club of a lot of my best friends back home in Scandinavia so it was a special game for me in every respect.

The circumstances were special for United too because the week before they had lost 5-0 to their title rivals Newcastle at St James' Park and been totally outplayed. They were not used to letting in 11 goals in the space of a week.

It was also a year after the game at Southampton where they famously swapped their 'invisible' grey shirts at half-time so there was a lot of talk about that in the build-up both in our dressing room and in the media.

As a boy I supported United's arch rivals Liverpool. My dad gave me a Liverpool shirt when I was four so they were the first club I ever heard of and that also made it an even bigger occasion for me.

Names like Cantona – arguably the greatest foreign import in Premier League history – Peter Schmeichel and Roy Keane were players I had been watching on TV a couple of weeks before so it was a bit surreal being on the same pitch as them and beating them so convincingly.

Not that the superstar names on the opposition team-sheet bothered me much in the days and hours leading up to kick-off. Every game I have ever played, no matter where it has been or who against, I have always felt walking out onto the pitch I can win.

Keane was sent off very early in the game and that certainly helped us because at the beginning of the match it was very even.

The fiery Irishman was always a very volatile opponent but in my view to get two bookings within 20 minutes, as he did that day, you are not doing your job for the team.

Keane had already been shown a yellow card for dissent when he needlessly chopped down Claus Lundekvam in the middle of the pitch so could have no complaints about the dismissal.

I think that was more a problem with Keane's mentality than an example of the United players being fired up because of what happened the season before.

Ferguson had rested one or two big names because they were involved in the Champions League so the culmination of when we saw the team sheet, the result the week before and Keane's red card made us even more confident.

We were already 1-0 up by the time Keane was given his marching orders as Eyal Berkovic had got us off to a dream start by opening the scoring with only six minutes played.

I had a big part to play in the goal because Eyal hammered in the rebound after the great Schmeichel had beaten away my initial shot from a tight angle.

Matt Le Tissier sent the home fans wild ten minutes before half-time with a superb solo goal, chipping the ball over the giant Schmeichel from the edge of the box, as Philippe Albert had done for Newcastle days earlier.

The goal was typical Le Tiss. I have played with a lot of great players over the years but his talent was unbelievable.

He used to do those kind of things all the time in training, which infuriated our own goalkeepers. Keepers are a unique bunch and hate being lobbed so if ever he tried it and succeeded they would boot the ball into the bushes and make him go and fetch it.

Matt's technique, touch and his finishing were sensational. There is no doubt he had the raw talent but was lacking other important ingredients required to become one of the best players of his generation in England.

In terms of football smartness there was nobody out there who was even close to him, but he just did not have that hunger and fitness you need in the modern game.

That is why he never left Southampton; a combination of loyalty and what he wanted to do with his career.

Matt was in contention for the England squad for France 98. He played in a B international against Russia before the World Cup and scored a hat-trick so I think he was close to making it.

Glenn Hoddle, the national coach, always liked him and tried to sign him when he was at Chelsea but controversially left him out of the squad at the last minute.

Matt was not envious of me playing in the tournament. He was not too unhappy to miss out on the World Cup and spent the summer playing golf. Maybe that is why he never played much for England. He was happy with what he had at Southampton.

Southampton was, and still is, compared to other teams, a small club and in the Premier League era there has only ever been one big, big star and that was Le Tiss. He was a fantastic guy. He was a big fish in a very small pond but the way he was towards me and every other player, very down to earth and helpful. He was a great guy and he could so easily have been totally different because of his status at the club.

David Beckham had scored from the halfway line against Wimbledon on the opening day of that season and he pulled one back for United from a trademark free-kick before I banged in my first goal to restore our two-goal lead going into the break.

That goal was set up by a fantastic left-wing run from Berkovic, who was a great player in the year we played together. He and I had a great understanding and we clicked straight away.

Eyal is a stubborn little thing and knows what he wants. He was a big star in Israel so he had a bit of an attitude which rubbed some people up the wrong way but he and I were close.

We didn't spent much time together off the pitch but he liked me and I liked him. We shared rooms when we went to away games.

Eyal gave me the ball and I cut in past David May. It was a really tight angle and I decided to smash the ball as hard as I could against the near post and it went in. It was a good finish.

May made amends for any blame attached to him by making it 3-2 from another Beckham free-kick only for Eyal to claim his second goal and our fourth of a topsy-turvy contest.

The United defence made a hash of clearing a Le Tissier corner from the left and when the ball fell to Eyal on the edge of the box he thumped a stunning volley into the top corner. It was another beautiful goal.

Eyal and I combined once again for my second goal when he played me in down the left with a pinpoint through ball which sent me one-on-one with Schmeichel so I rolled the ball past him and into the far corner.

For the third I found myself all on my own against Schmeichel again so I decided to dribble around his outstretched left boot before side-footing the ball into an unguarded net.

Just as the ball crossed the line Neville slid in, in a desperate bid to try and keep it out and got the slightest touch but my shot was goal-bound anyway so it was definitely my goal.

It seems crazy to think one month before I had been marvelling at what a brilliant goalkeeper Schmeichel was but when you are out there and caught up in the moment you don't think about who you are playing against.

It is a tactical decision. You have to decide if you going to go for power, placement or try and chip the goalkeeper and in that situation it does not matter if it is Schmeichel in goal or my wife!

Paul Scholes bundled in a consolation goal for United in between my second and third strikes but it was not enough to spare the visitors' blushes.

Two of my Norway team-mates Ronnie Johnsen and Ole Gunnar Solskjaer had just arrived at United. Ole came on as substitute so I had a chat to him after the game.

He was right at the beginning of what would be a glittering career at United, including scoring the winner in the last minute of the 1999 European Cup Final, so I am sure the result was a bit of a shock to him.

I think United were hoping and expecting to get back to their usual winning form after being embarrassed by Newcastle the week before. They did not see this result coming and neither did we.

The United players were not interested in swapping shirts at full time and they definitely did not want to sign my match ball. They are not used to losing two games in a row by big scorelines like that; they were not happy.

Graeme Souness was our manager at the time and he was always very good in those last couple of minutes before you walk out of the tunnel at boosting your confidence.

He used to talk a lot about the key factor in the success of the great Liverpool team he was a part of in the 80s, which we all remember as a great passing team.

Souness said it was not their football that set Liverpool apart from their rivals at home and in Europe but it was was about the mentality to go out and win the war.

He said, 'Sometimes we won the war after ten minutes, sometimes after 89 minutes.' He also used to tell us to go out and play good football and remember we were playing in a great league and to treasure the moment.

As a player it is not always easy to do that when you are caught up in the heat of battle because that is your everyday life.

I think Graeme was very keen on beating United and Ferguson because of his Anfield connections and we had seen the week before, even though Newcastle had a great team, it was possible. We felt it was a good time to play them.

I owe Graeme a huge debt of gratitude because he was the one who gave me my chance in the Premier League but I have mixed feelings about him as a manager having also played for him at Blackburn after departing the south coast.

I had a very good season at Stavanger when Saints signed me. The Norwegian league ran from April to November so we were coming to the end of our season.

Southampton had seen me in quite a few games and I was just breaking into the national team and scoring a lot of goals.

They invited me over, I trained with them for a couple of days to have a look at the club and luckily they wanted to offer me a contract.

I always say that when Souness was my manager at Southampton I could not do anything wrong and when he was my manager at Blackburn I could not do anything right because the two of us did not see eye-to-eye at Ewood Park.

The truth is I did not only play good games at Southampton and was not always bad at Blackburn, but any player will tell you confidence is a big thing in football and if you have a manager that really believes in you and shows he believes in you it is amazing how well you can do.

At Blackburn I was in the totally opposite situation to when we were together at Southampton but his approach to the job was very different to when our paths crossed for a second time.

At Southampton he was more active when it came to coaching than he was at Blackburn, probably because there was no money to spend. Bringing in more players was not an option so he had to make the best out of what he had.

I also learnt very early on that Souness was not a man to be messed with.

He always used to join in training on Fridays when we would play a match among ourselves and I recall one situation with Dave Beasant, our goalkeeper, after Souness had dropped him from the team.

It was clear to everyone the manager didn't rate him and wanted to bring in a new number one and he signed Chris Woods soon after I came, which big Bez was not happy about.

The goalkeepers also used to join in these training matches and on this particular day everybody knew Bez was out to get Souness in that game.

Souness was not stupid and he knew as well so in the middle of the contest the ball was in between them and they were both going at it.

Neither of them were looking at the ball, they were just smashing into each other. Beasant fell to the ground and Souness trampled all over him.

Bez was covered in cuts from head-to-toe afterwards so you can say Souness, a fierce competitor in his own playing days, won that little duel.

I have fond memories of playing at The Dell. The atmosphere was always great because basically the crowd was sitting on the pitch.

There were just over 15,000 people there to watch this game, they made a lot of noise. I guess it was a bit surreal for them too watching their unfancied team thrash the country's best so I was in good company.

There were a lot of tight corridors at The Dell and the away dressing room was quite a long way from the home one but we had the same entrance so we could see all those great United players walking past us on their way into the ground, a far cry from their luxurious Old Trafford surroundings.

Before we went out onto the pitch a group of us with Le Tiss in charge had a little game of keep-ups in the dressing room just to keep any pre-match nerves under control.

Le Tiss had an alternative warm-up to the rest of us; he basically went out before the game, shot the ball towards the goal four or five times and then went back into the changing room.

Jason Dodd was very lively in the build-up to a match and was a great character. Le Tiss was not as loud as Doddsy but was good to be around in the run-up to a match.

We also had Jim Magilton at the time who was a very loud Northern Irishman. In fact I have never played with a player who talked as much as him before and during a game.

He was always moaning about one thing or another but was another good guy.

Robbie Slater, a talented young Australian winger who had a championship winner's medal from his days at Blackburn, was pretty noisy as well so we had a very lively dressing room.

The mood in training the Monday after the game was naturally very good and we had a great group of players at the time with a good camaraderie. We were quite close as team-mates so it was a nice environment for Claus Lundekvam, my fellow countryman and I, and the other new arrivals to come into.

Claus is a very relaxed person, honest and with him there are no hidden agendas in any way. He is just a nice guy, sometimes too nice and a little bit too naïve.

He wants to be good to everyone all the time and sadly there are some people that will take advantage and he has experienced that.

Claus signed a short time before me and I had played against him in Norway and alongside him for the national team, but before we were thrown together at Southampton I did not know him well.

We stayed in the same hotel and spent a lot of time together, especially at the beginning so we became very close.

Unfortunately, as has been well documented, Claus's partying spiralled out of control but at that time it was nice to come to a new club and a new country where there is someone there you can act Norwegian with.

Claus's biggest strength as a player was he was very good at reading the game.

I remember Souness compared him a bit to his former Liverpool team-mate Alan Hansen and he is that type of player, very quick with a brilliant football brain.

He is a long, thin thing and when you were against him in training you always came away hurting.

He was not a dirty or malicious player but he had bones sticking out everywhere.

I think he is still very high up in the list of most appearances in the Premier League by a foreign player so that shows he had an amazing career at Southampton.

It always helps you settle at a new club when you do well at the beginning so things could not have gone any better for me in those first few weeks. Scoring a hat-trick against a team of the stature of United earns you respect in the dressing room straight away.

All the players spent quite a bit of time together away from training and we had guys like Dodd, Magilton and Le Tiss who were good at making sure the players stayed together.

We never missed an opportunity to go out and let our hair down, although there were some people who found more opportunities than others.

There were quite a few good drinkers at the club and we enjoyed ourselves when there was a time for doing that.

At that time there was probably more of a drinking culture than there is these days but we were sensible most of the time!

Our favourite haunt was Ocean Village where there was a bar called Los Marinos and another in the city centre called the Square Balloon where we were regular visitors. I can remember spending many hours at those two establishments. I always found drinking together can be good for morale and that can help performances on the pitch.

I cannot remember what time I got home the night of the United match but it is fair to say Southampton was a happy place to be that evening.

A few of us went out for a meal and some beers and I drank quite a few pints of Newcastle Brown Ale.

One of the coaching staff, Alan Murray, was with us and I think I got a gold star from him because he did not expect this to be the chosen drink for someone with my Scandinavian roots. Souness was quite relaxed about what we got up to as long as we played and trained as we should.

As I have already mentioned, I have the match ball as a memento of the game and although my football stuff is very well hidden in my house it is a nice thing to keep.

It is nice to get the ball out every couple of years and remind some of my United-supporting friends what I did against their beloved club.

They were as surprised as me that I scored a hat-trick. I guess they were thinking 'well if it is as easy as that, maybe I should became a professional'.

In a bizarre way I am better known in Norway because I scored three goals against United than for the goals I scored against our local clubs that got me the move to Southampton in the first place.

There are not many Norwegians who have scored more Premier League goals than I did so if I had only been a top player in Norway I would not be as famous.

I was also part of the best Norwegian team in our history. We would go on to beat Brazil at the 1998 World Cup, a result that shocked the sporting world.

But even now all anybody wants to talk to me about is that United game. I am just grateful they don't ask me about the games that followed as we lost 7-1 at Everton a couple of weeks later so I guess we were not that great after all.

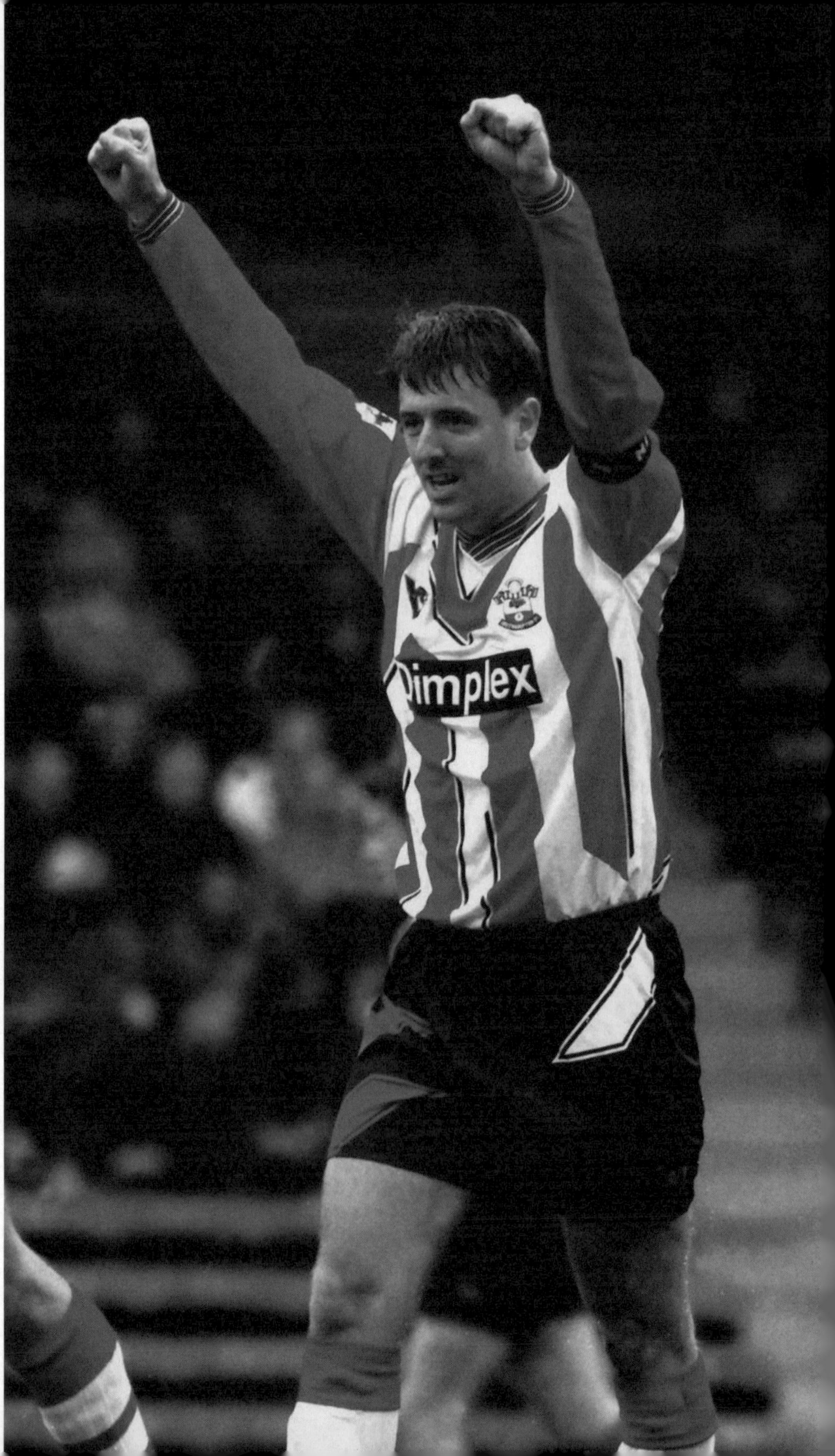
Dimplex

Matt Le Tissier

Southampton 2 (Le Tissier 2)

Newcastle 1 (Cole)

Premier League
The Dell, Sunday 24 October 1993

Southampton: Flowers, Kenna, Wood, Moore, (Moody, 77), Benali, Adams, Maddison, Reid, Allen, Le Tissier, Dowie

LOOKING BACK on it this performance was a massive turning point in my career as it was not really going anywhere at that point.

Playing under Ian Branfoot, if anything, I had gone backwards as a player and this game changed everything for me as it was my first back after being dropped for five matches.

It was live on Sky Sports which made it all the more special as it really made people sit up and take note of me again.

It was said afterwards that the first goal was one finger up to Branny and the winning goal was the second finger. That made me laugh.

I scored a lot of goals I am very proud of in my career but to bag two spectacular ones in the same match was very special and is the reason this game stands out for me and is my favourite.

It was not only a big game for the club but in terms of what had happened, with me getting the elbow, to come back and make this statement was important.

Although I don't think I would have left the club if I hadn't got back in the team and showed my capabilities as I realised at that point the manager would not be around much longer.

I did not have to stick in a transfer request or anything as you could feel he was under so much pressure it couldn't have gone on for the rest of the season.

He was struggling to win over the fans and crowd numbers had started to dwindle; once that happens as a manager you have not got much time left.

Having said that I am sure Branny looks back on it now and thinks what a great managerial decision it was to drop me as I went on to have the best spell of my career.

But it was only after he got sacked in January and Alan Ball came in that I enjoyed a scintillating five month spell resulting in me winning Saints' Player of the Year award for the second time and finishing the season with 25 goals. It turned out to not be a bad year in the end after a dreadful start and going into this match we were in serious trouble, having won just one of our opening 11 games in the league.

I had been left out of the previous three Premier League games and two cup ties with the manager not even naming me in the squad. I was top scorer at the time so it was not a nice position to be in.

Branny's style of play was not really suited to the way I wanted to play football so there was always going to be a bit of a clash.

He thought I didn't work hard enough in his system, but that was the point. I wanted, when I got the ball, to try to create things and not be robotic and programmed to hit the ball in a certain area if I picked it up in a specific position.

It was just so basic and so easy to defend against and not my style. We had completely different ideas on how football should be played and it was a long two-and-a-half years when he was in charge. Considering all this though and the position we were in for him to drop me as top scorer was a bit strange.

From my point of view I did not think I was playing badly enough to be pulled from the squad completely. It was all a bit odd.

I did not argue and there were no major rows between us as I was not the confrontational type of player.

It was his decision and I accepted it. He handed me back to Dave Merrington in the reserves and said 'go and get him right and do whatever you can to get him back to top form'.

Dave had been my old youth team manager and we just went back to doing sessions based around me getting the ball and being positive, taking players on and getting my confidence back.

It was not to do with fitness, they just wanted me back playing in a positive frame of mind and doing the things I was good at. That is everything we had worked at when I was a young player.

I do not think my team-mates were particularly shocked when it was first announced I was not in the squad as they probably knew it was only a matter of time. It was inevitable at some point Branny would not want me in his team, but those are the ups and downs of being a footballer and you take the good with the bad.

Paul Moody came in to replace me but it was not awkward between us at all as he is the nicest person you could ever wish to meet.

I suppose it is a bit funny looking back at it now and it is quite difficult to believe considering the careers we both went on to have that he would have been preferred to me for a few games. He is probably the first lad who would admit it, to be honest.

I have nothing against him, we were all team-mates and when the manager decides he wants to play someone else there is nothing you can do about it, you just get on with it without moaning.

Luckily for me we did not have a particularly good spell of results in my absence, drawing two very winnable league games and losing to Arsenal, so that helped my cause. We even got knocked out by Shrewsbury 2-0 in the League Cup at their ground and I think that might have been the final straw to bring me back in as the travelling faithful really gave Branny some stick.

I was fully aware the fans were on his back as they made it pretty clear they wanted me playing again in the next game.

The way it all transpired it actually made my bond with our supporters even stronger with the fact this game was my first back from being dropped and it all going so well.

It was the fans who were one of the main reasons why I never left the club as they were brilliant with me from the day I made my debut.

As has been well documented, I was close to going when I nearly joined my boyhood club Tottenham when I was 21. Liverpool were also interest in 1992 and Chelsea in 1995 but I never had any regrets about staying.

I was very young back then and didn't think it was the right thing to do and the fans always made me feel so wanted on the south coast.

It was bizarre when they used to stand up and bow to me when I took a corner. I think it was something they picked up from a film and it caught on but I didn't have a clue what they were doing at first.

I spent a lot of time on the bench in my first couple of years as a professional as Chris Nicholl didn't think I could last 90 minutes so he would use me as an impact substitute.

Whenever I was on the bench they always sung my name and encouraged Chris to get me on the pitch.

I don't think they realise how much influence it has on a player when they are so supportive of them and how much it lifts them, they certainly did that with me.

I had an inkling on the Friday, two days before we played Newcastle on the Sunday, that I was back in the starting XI.

We started working on some team shape in training with me playing just off Iain Dowie, and you had an idea if you were included in the first set of drills the manager would probably be going with you.

Newcastle were flying at the time and had a lot of good players who made them a real attacking force, not that I would be doing much defending but it was important to get some points on the board.

Branny didn't say anything in the dressing room beforehand or have any special words of wisdom for me.

It was almost as if he was begrudging me my place back in the team, like it wasn't him that wanted me to play but he had to as the fans were baying for his blood.

I went through my own usual pre-match warm-up to get ready. They used to be brilliant. For most of my career, until the mid to late 90s, we were responsible for our own routines.

I would just take shots at goal from all over the place and then go in between the sticks myself and get all the lads to take shots at me. It was so much fun.

Despite this I rarely got injured back in those days, funnily enough it was only later on in my career when I warmed up with the team I started to get knocks. Personally I think they should have left me alone.

It has been suggested I used to eat McDonalds before a game but this was always a myth. I would never do that. I used to have cheese omelette and baked beans. That was pretty standard until we started with the pasta.

I never actually ate McDonalds that much, I would have a breakfast from there on the way to training occasionally but not before a match.

Even with the game being live on TV I remember there being another great atmosphere inside The Dell. What a quirky and intimidating ground it was.

The fans were so close to the pitch and it created a brilliant noise. With the action being that close the opposition players did not feel comfortable as they could hear every bit of abuse that was thrown at them.

Also, it could not hold many away fans so they could never make much noise, which was good for us. It was always a good atmosphere in our favour down there.

I am sure some players would have gone out onto the pitch with a real 'I am going to show you' attitude, but that has never been my approach.

I was just pleased to head back into the stadium in front of a packed crowd instead of being with the reserves who played in front of one man and his dog.

That is what being a footballer is all about, stepping out onto the pitch with a full house willing you on and doing what you do best.

I certainly did not have any real angst towards Branny or think that I had to play well otherwise I would get left out again.

That was not how I motivated myself. I needed to be in a relaxed frame of mind to play to the best of my capabilities.

I missed a simple chance early on in the game. The ball came across me quite quickly in the box and I snatched at it, miss-hit it and Mike Hooper, the Newcastle goalkeeper, made an easy save. I was gutted as it would have been nice to get off to a good start.

Besides that effort I fluffed, the first half came and went in a blur but I would not have to wait long to get my name back on the scoresheet.

My opening goal is probably the second favourite of my career, behind the 35-yard strike against Blackburn when I lobbed it over my former team-mate and good pal Tim Flowers after dribbling around a couple of their players.

That one only sneaks it because on this occasion I scuffed the finish a bit at the end after I had done the tricks and got past a few defenders.

I went to side-foot the ball into the corner and really wanted it to be a nice crisp finish but I miscued the shot off the bottom of my boot and it trickled into the net.

As it happened Hooper was flat-footed anyway so it didn't matter but from a perfectionist point of view it would have been nice if I had struck it how I wanted.

I was not thinking about what I was doing, it all just happened on the spur of the moment and after the game all I could remember was the dodgy finish. In celebration I just had a little run off with my hand in the air and that was that.

It was not until I watched it back on the TV later that night I realised just how much I had done beforehand to get into as shooting position. I didn't realise at first how good a goal it was.

Before seeing the net bulge it is fair to say it wasn't all going my way up until that moment and I think I was very close to being hauled off moments before, although I was not aware of it during the match.

Moody had been sent out to warm up. I only saw this on the TV coverage afterwards when it showed the goal as the camera panned back to the bench and I lip-read Branny saying to him, 'sit down Moods'.

He was obviously going to bring him on. I had a fair idea it might have been in my place as the first hour of the game had not gone great.

Obviously there was a chance it could have been Dowie for all I know but the way things were back then I was certainly favourite to get the hook.

We were soon pegged back to one-all when the prolific Andy Cole equalised ten minutes later for his ninth goal of the season. That was not good news as we were the kind of team who liked to be in front.

When someone equalised we did not often fight back to take the lead again. It was almost like we would be on the back foot and defend to try and get a draw.

It was nice to actually go on and win the game as we were in a dire position and it was one-way traffic for Newcastle after they scored and Flowers had to make a few really good saves to keep us in it.

When we were under the cosh we managed an attack down the left and I played in Micky Adams, who was as fit as a butcher's dog and still making overlapping runs late in the game when other players would have been tiring, for a cross.

Micky whipped one in and the defender cleared the ball to Neil Maddison, who just headed it on to me. I was knackered at that point as it was the 87th minute.

I was struggling for a bit of air and after controlling the ball with my thigh it just fell perfectly for me to hit on the volley. It was instinct.

I took it on my thigh, set myself up for the volley and as soon as it left my foot I knew it had a chance, but it was not until the last second I realised it was going in.

From my angle I wasn't sure the ball was going to dip enough underneath the crossbar but it turns out it was nowhere near the bar so I am not sure why I was worrying.

That strike is definitely up there in my top ten goals as well and both of them went on to win first and second prize in the Premier League's October goal of the month competition, which was a great achievement. I am not sure that had ever been done by one player before.

It was also nice to finally get the three points on the board and that second goal came late enough in the game for us to hold on to our lead.

After the final whistle Branny might have patted me on the back and said 'well done' but it was still very early on in the season so no one got ahead of ourselves.

It was not one of those where you won and knew you were staying in the league so could have a big party after. We still had a lot of work to be done.

The lads in the dressing room were buzzing though and that was the thing that got us through most of the time.

Sometimes we did not really have the most talented squad and there were teams who got relegated who had better players than we did but the spirit and camaraderie was always unbelievably good.

Of the team that day, Tim and Franny Benali were my best mates and it was a shame when Tim left for Blackburn as he was a funny boy and a good lad, he was definitely missed as he was such a good goalkeeper.

I wasn't a party animal and didn't really drink alcohol at that time, that started a bit later on in my career, so I generally used to go home and chill out with my family after games.

Three months later Branny got the boot. I was pleased when he left but of course it is not nice when a manager loses his job and as a bloke I felt for him and what he went through. Some of the protests that went on were a bit out of order.

But from a career point of view, on the day he got the sack, I was not disappointed.

Alan Ball came in and what he did was very simple. He literally built the team around me. He put me in the middle of the pitch and said to the other players 'this is your best chance of getting out of trouble, he is the best player at the football club, whenever you get the ball the first thing I want you to do is to pass to him'.

It made me feel a million dollars. To have a manager who has that much belief in me sent me to another level as a footballer and sent my confidence through the roof. I got 45 goals in 64 games under Bally.

These included two vital hat-tricks against Norwich and Liverpool towards the end of the 1993/94 season, which have also stayed in my mind.

The goals came from me playing in the little pocket behind the forwards and it was unusual from what I had experienced under Branny who didn't really want me in his team.

From a personal point of view the time under Bally was the best of my career although my favourite time off the field was in the 1989/90 season playing with fellow guys from the youth team like Franny, Alan Shearer and the Wallace brothers.

From a poor position in the table when Bally came in we finished 18th and just one point off the relegation zone. Those two goals turned out to be two of my most important when you look back.

We could have gone down on the final day but got a point against West Ham in 3-3 draw with me scoring twice. I netted eight goals in the last six games as we picked up ten points to stay in the league.

The final day games I never looked at as high pressured. I enjoyed it. It is not nice to be in those positions in the first place but to have so much riding on that one match to get the points to stay up was a scenario I relished.

I looked at it in the sense that it was a massive game for the football club and a chance for me to be a hero and score the goal to keep us up.

I think people who go into those games not looking forward to them are the ones who don't perform and get relegated, the ones who embrace it and take the positives are the ones who normally do well.

We stayed up by the skin of our teeth for so many seasons and it was very difficult to see the club end up in League One for a spell. We went through some really awful years.

But my connection with the fans and love for the club has never, and will never, die despite some unsavoury events.

In more recent years I was never actually banned from St Mary's. I was just not made welcome at the stadium. It could have been worse, Franny was actually banned.

It was not nice but it never dulled my enthusiasm to go and support Southampton whenever I could and champion their cause on the TV.

It was one of those things, Franny and I are both adults and understood the type of bloke Nicola Cortese was.

We could not fight or beat it so just accepted it as we knew it would change and the football club will be there longer than any individual, as Branfoot found to his cost all those years earlier.

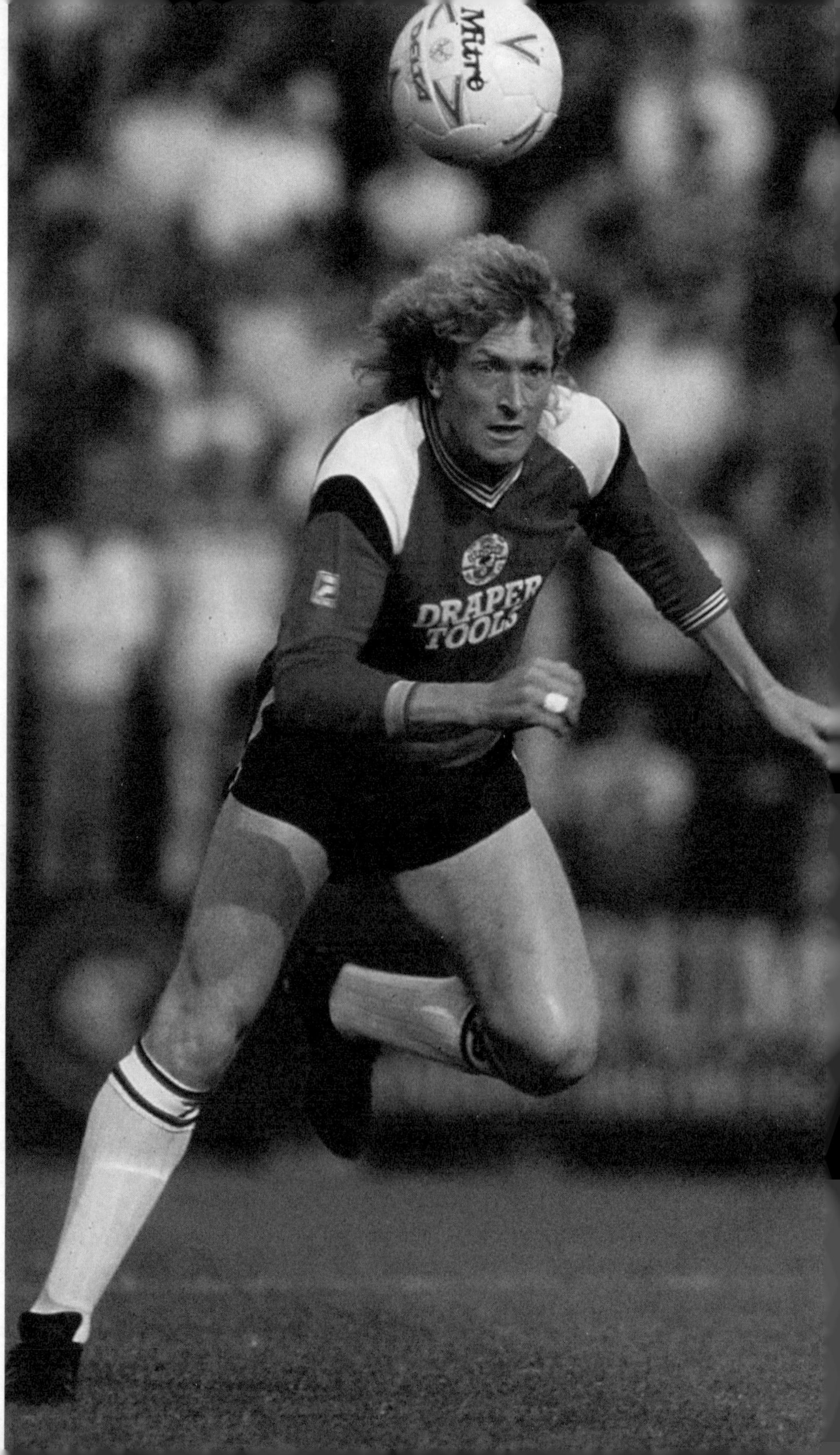

GLENN COCKERILL

Glenn Cockerill

Nottingham Forest 3 (Gemmill 2, Black)
Southampton 2 (Le Tissier, Moore)

Zenith Data Systems Cup Final
Wembley, Sunday 29 March 1992

Southampton: Flowers, Kenna, Moore, Ruddock, Benali, Cockerill, Horne, Hurlock, Le Tissier, Shearer, Dowie

IT WAS at the moment I was walking the lads out at Wembley in front of more than 68,000 fans, I knew all my years of hard graft had paid off.

Another boyhood dream of mine had come true. The first one was to be a professional footballer and I had to work hard enough just to achieve that.

When I finally made it with Lincoln at the age of 17, it took me almost ten years to get to the top and sign for Southampton; to play at the home of English football was my next target.

Obviously, you want to play for your national side but the next best thing is turning out at Wembley with a club you love.

It is one thing playing at the national stadium but it is a whole other experience altogether walking out first with the captain's armband on.

I had been there on a school trip once before when I was a young kid, we went to watch a home international, although I can't remember who against, and I was fascinated.

I said to myself I would do everything possible to make sure the next time I went back would be as a player.

The fact I eventually achieved it meant so much as I thought my chance with a big club like Southampton had possibly gone.

In my first year we nearly did it when we got to the semi-final of the FA Cup in 1986 but we were beaten by Liverpool.

We were close on a couple of other occasions under Chris Nicholl but it wasn't to be and I was starting to think it had passed me by.

It may not have been the FA Cup but it was a competition we all took very seriously and really wanted to win especially as the final was at Wembley.

I wanted to win every game we played, whether it is in training or on a match-day. Even now I play with my young children in the garden and still want to beat them, I will never lose that.

This game is all the more memorable for me as I had had a difficult season. For most of my career at Saints I had been an ever present unless I was injured.

I started the season under Ian Branfoot as captain until January, when we were beaten 2-1 by Everton on New Year's Day. The result ensured we had only won once in nine league games.

The manager dropped me afterwards and I was heartbroken. He said, 'you are trying to do too much, you are backing everybody, just stay out of the team and have a rest'.

I had not been used to that and it hurt. I was determined to get back into the team even though I was not as young as I once was.

One of the reasons I so wanted my place back was I had this feeling after the second round tie with Bristol City in October that we were going to get to Wembley and win a cup.

Something was just telling me that with Ian getting a lot of stick off the fans for dropping Matt Le Tissier and letting Jimmy Case leave, we may just achieve something.

Blimey, did Ian take some flack for getting rid of Jim, but from what I heard that decision was not made by him but other people higher up in the club.

Ian and myself went back a long way. When I signed for Lincoln in 1976 he was a player at the club and I lived in digs around the corner from him.

I never kept in touch with him when he left, and the next time I heard his name was when he was announced as the manager of Southampton.

It took a while to get to know him and get on with him again but he was a fair man. He had to make decisions and could not please everybody.

Even Tiss won't be able to say he was not an honest person or nasty to work with.

Of course, I fell out with him and we had a bit of an argument when he left me out but as I was a senior professional and captain I respected him and worked hard to get my place back.

Looking back on it, maybe I was not performing as I should have been. I might have looked tired but as a footballer you never use that as an excuse.

He might have been right as I was trying very hard to do everything correctly in my captaincy duties with the players off the pitch.

I was arranging for them to open school fetes and shops and was probably organising too much when I shouldn't have done. Fair play to the gaffer as after he dropped me we only lost two out of the next 12 games in the league!

When I eventually got recalled it was not for the reasons I would have wanted as my best mate in the side Micky Adams, who had been playing superbly, got injured before the final.

These things happen in football and on the one hand I was delighted and grateful to be playing, but on the other my heart went out to Mick.

So much so that after I received the runners-up medal I went straight to Mick and offered it to him. I said, 'I know it is a losing one but I wouldn't have played if you hadn't been injured.' Mick told me not to be silly and to keep it but I think he appreciated the gesture.

This showed the togetherness of the squad and spirit we had as a bunch of players at the time and it was helped by Ian's good man-management skills.

That was one of Ian's strong points and before the final we went up to London and two nights before the match Ian took us all out to see 'Buddy' the musical in the West End.

It was a great idea and everyone really enjoyed it as it relaxed us all and got us bonding together.

He got us all together and enjoying each other's company. When we went out for a pint, we all went, and anyone who didn't would get fined by me!

The guys were as good as gold to keep in order. Francis Benali would never drink so would hold the whip, which was the most important job. You couldn't have left all the money with too many of my team-mates believe me.

Franny was one of the sensible ones when we went on tour and came in very handy as by the end of the night no one would know where the money was as we were too drunk.

Like a knight in shining armour, Franny would pop up with the cash still left and sort it out.

I was not afraid to have a beer or two before a big match and my pre-game routine was to sink a couple of pints before bed the night before.

Jimmy Case and I roomed together for six years before he left and we would, without fail, have a couple of beers on the evening before every match.

It is one of those things I got into as it relaxed me and didn't affect my performance the next day so I stuck with it.

I had no trouble going to sleep before taking on Brian Clough's men, who it must be said, I classed as our nemesis.

They had beaten us in the fourth round of the League Cup earlier in the season and also ended our run in the FA Cup the previous campaign in a fifth-round replay.

We were maybe a bit closer matched this time around and they no doubt wanted revenge after an Alan Shearer strike and two Tiss goals saw us run out 3-1 winners at their place earlier in the season.

They had a few injuries but still possessed players like Roy Keane, Teddy Sheringham, Nigel Clough and Stuart Pearce, not that we feared any of them.

Despite us being in the away changing room it was still on a different level to that of The Dell. Playing at the stadium was a massive culture shock for most of us.

There was a good atmosphere pre-match with all the lads getting on well with each other. I had a great sense of pride to be leading them out.

Before the game I remember the captains, myself and Pearce, and the two managers going to meet in the rest-room to hand over the team sheets.

Cloughie had obviously had a few drinks as his nose was getting redder and redder by the minute but he was a top manager and it was a pleasure to be in his company before the match.

We swapped pleasantries and line-ups before getting on with our own jobs.

I would be face-to-face once more with Pearce sooner than I expected but it would be him making the early journey back to the changing rooms.

In a match report afterwards it was said my most telling contribution to the occasion was when I flew into the tackle with Stuart in the first minute and left him with damaged knee ligaments.

His injury was nothing to do with any malice or a bad lunge on my part. It was early in the game and it was a 50/50 ball.

Like Stuart, I have never shirked away from anybody on the pitch. He was going to play the ball down the line and it was there to be won. I block-tackled him and went through with everything I had.

He got up limping but true to his spirit, tried to carry on before being replaced by Steve Chettle on 19 minutes. He didn't say anything to me about it, he never did chat and I always found him a bit miserable to be honest.

Funnily enough Tim Flowers, who was our goalkeeper that day and worked with Stuart at Manchester City, used to take the mickey out of him for going off the pitch.

Tim would say to him, 'you are no psycho, our skipper sorted you out no problem at all'. Hearing that amused me! It was obviously a shame for him as he hobbled down the tunnel but it was a plus for us as they had to reshuffle their team and I thought it may have just been our day.

We changed our positions around as well when Stuart went off with me and Tiss switching wings.

Initially our mercurial number seven had not wanted to play against Stuart as he would have kicked him off the park so I took him on instead.

I relished the battle and used to study the opponent in the week leading up to the match and work out how I could get the better of them.

Us swapping worked and Tiss started to get into the game but we were left bitterly disappointed when they went into a two-nil lead. We could not get going for the opening 30 minutes and the damage was done by half-time.

Scot Gemmill got their first after 15 minutes with a quite brilliant strike. Roy Keane flicked on a Gary Crosby throw-in and Gemmill was on hand to volley it past Tim from 15 yards.

We were being dominated and Nigel Clough had two chances to extend their advantage but could not find a way past Tim.

It was a cruel blow losing the second goal just before the break as we had just started to find our way and string a few passes together.

Gemmill played a defence-splitting pass for Kingsley Black to race onto and fire into the back of the net from 20 yards. We barely even had time to take the restart.

In the dressing room Ian drilled it into us that we were not out of the game as we had shown we could create chances.

It could have been a nightmare going 2-0 down and, on other occasions, it could have gone on to be a rout but we looked at it another way and were determined not to let that happen.

We knew we had a lot of people up in the stands watching us who we would have to see afterwards and we didn't want it to be an embarrassment.

I had sorted out tickets for all of my family to come down and watch me. It was a huge day for my dad, Ron, who was also a professional for 18 years. He was a proud man seeing his eldest son leading a side out at Wembley.

The experienced lads all knew even at 2-0 we had a chance if we showed the right attitude. We would never lie down and were aware the next goal was the important one.

We rode our luck at times though and the game could have gotten away from us. Tim somehow saved a header from Sheringham before keeping out Black minutes later.

What a shot-stopper and fantastic all-round number one Tim was. He was only 25 at this point, young for a goalie, but showed maturity beyond his years to deal with everything thrown at him.

Maturity is not one thing you would normally associate with him off the pitch though as he always liked to have the last laugh and was a very comical guy to have around the place.

Keane should have made it 3-0 on the hour but blasted over when well-placed and Tim had to deny Gary Crosby before we got back in it.

When the goal came I thought we looked so strong and from that moment I was sure there was only going to be one winner.

It was no surprise it was Tiss who got us back in the game after 64 minutes when he got in ahead of Des Walker to head a Neil Ruddock cross past Andy Marriott.

I thought it was fitting he should score as he had bagged six goals in five games, including a hat-trick against Chelsea in the semi-final, to help us reach the promised land.

Our young striker Alan Shearer had also been in fine form, netting three times en route to Wembley.

Tiss was a pleasure to watch as he had a fantastic natural talent and at the time you wouldn't have thought Alan would do better internationally than him.

Watching them grow up, get better and improve you would have said Tiss would be the one to go on to bigger and better things.

But Shearer had a different attitude, he was a bit like myself in how he would work and graft. He had a fantastic knack for scoring goals and deserved everything he got.

I have got closer to Tiss since we finished playing, maybe as I don't have to do his running anymore.

He was a talent of his own different kind and in the period when Alan Ball came in as manager he was the best footballer Southampton have ever had.

He was heavily involved in us pulling it back to 2-2 with 20 minutes left on the clock when he whipped in a teasing corner that was met by the head of Kevin Moore.

The atmosphere after we equalised went up a notch or two. It turned into a cracking end-to-end contest and we had a right good go at it.

Some finals at the new Wembley since the famous Twin Towers were bulldozed have been very dull but that never seemed to happen at the old ground.

Shearer forced a save from Marriott before Iain Dowie shot narrowly wide as we pushed for the winner to complete an unlikely comeback.

We fancied ourselves whether in extra time or if it went to penalties. If it did go to spot-kicks with Alan and Tiss in the side we would have been hard to beat.

The game finished 2-2, and in the resulting 30 minutes I never felt like we would concede but after 112 minutes, disaster struck.

Gary Charles sent in a cross and Gemmill, who else, popped up unmarked at the far post to score the winner. Needless to say I was distraught.

We had eight minutes to throw the kitchen sink at them, which we did, but just ran out of time to get back on level terms once again.

Cloughie made his way to the dressing room by himself a happy man while we took part in a lap of honour to show our appreciation to the flocks of fans dressed in red and white who had travelled to north London.

With Stuart not around, Des Walker lifted the cup and I did have some jealously. I honestly felt the trophy was meant for me that year.

The dressing room was not the happiest of places for a while afterwards but we had a huge sense of satisfaction in our second-half display.

Our never-say-die attitude had won us a lot of plaudits and our big characters stood up to be counted.

It was also nice that one of those characters was Moore, who I had known since I was a young lad in Grimsby. We played in the same Grimsby Boys' team so it was amazing to then be playing at Wembley together.

The team that day was very different to the side I joined in 1985 with the likes of Peter Shilton, Nick Holmes, Mark Dennis and Steve Moran.

It was quite a transitional period. When I signed it was brilliant for me, after spending ten years in the lower leagues, to be training with these superstars. I felt like a kid at Christmas.

It was great being a footballer for Southampton. I can't put into words how much I loved it and never wanted it to be over.

I worked my socks off and stayed for nine happy seasons. I must have put some serious yards in as I have had two hip replacements since I have retired but it was all worth it.

I was not the most gifted player in the world but I knew how to stop opponents and score a goal. My application and drive was that I had a desire to be the best player in the team and on some days I was, and on others I was not.

But my record at the club shows not many players got in ahead of me in the starting XI. In more than 270 league appearances, only 15 of them were from the bench.

I actually felt sorry for some of the younger lads like Neil Maddison who could not budge me for a long time.

I kept my place after the cup final defeat and went on to play a big part in us avoiding relegation that year.

The very next game was against Everton at Goodison Park just three days later on the Wednesday night.

I scored the winner which took us to 40 points and more or less sealed our survival in the top flight.

We had quickly forgotten about the lows of Wembley and were buzzing to know we would still be first division footballers the following season as at one point it had not looked too promising.

The buzz I got on a Saturday from football was everything I lived for. Being part of a team and going into training at Saints was the most enjoyable period of my career.

I count myself very fortunate to have represented the club and have to thank Nicholl enormously for that.

It is down to him that I got the chance at the club. He was great for me, had faith in me and a lot of my career was down to him.

I think it was because I gave him the run around once when he was at Grimsby and I played at Sheffield United. That was why he signed me and I can't thank him enough. This final remains one of my favourite memories of my spell on the south coast. Hearing the roar of noise from our supporters as we made our way into the arena gave me goosebumps and will stay with me for ever.

I tried so hard to remember everything about the day as I was aware it may have been my last taste of an occasion like that. I wanted to soak every little thing up.

Thank God I did as it has helped me greatly when I was asked to contribute to this book.

We may not have won but if you had told the kid on a school trip who was lost in his own little world watching England play, that one day he would captain a top-flight side at the stadium in a cup final, he never would have believed you.

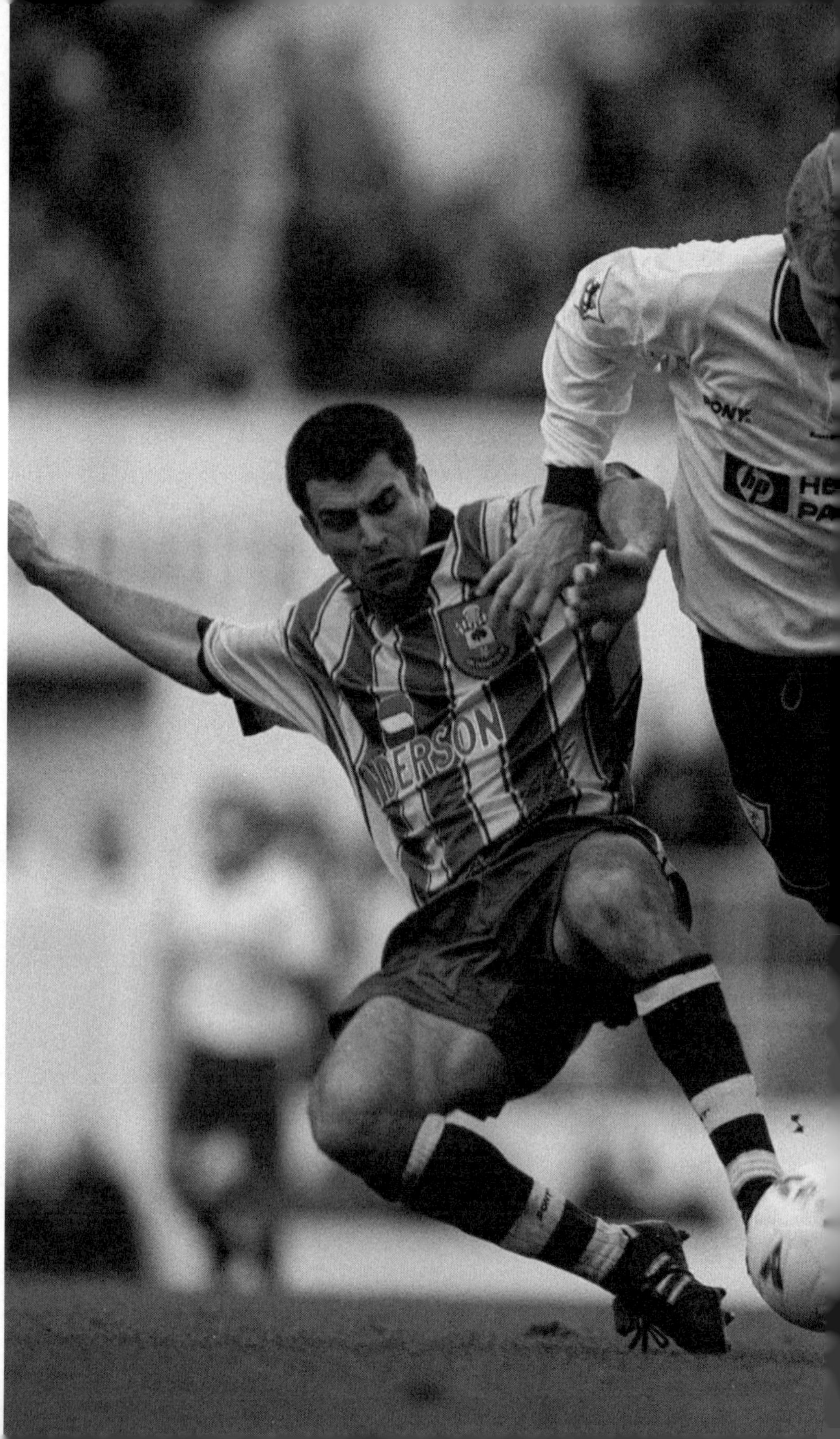

FRANCIS BENALI

Francis Benali

Southampton 4 (Rideout 2, Wallace, Le Tissier)
Liverpool 1 (Beardsley pen)

League Division One
The Dell, Saturday 21 October 1989

Southampton: Flowers, Dodd, Osman, Ruddock, Benali, Cockerill, Case, Le Tissier, Rideout, Wallace, Shearer (Baker, 70)

MUCH HAS been written about Manchester United's famous 'class of 92' – they even had a film made about them – but I believe the Saints team that hammered the then-mighty Liverpool would have been more than a match for David Beckham and co.

What made this game special was so many of us had graduated from the youth team together and, as a result, shared a unique bond.

If anything the scoreline flattered Liverpool because we hit the woodwork twice and should have won by more. It was such a one-sided victory.

Every time we attacked there was a good possibility we were going to score and games like that do not happen too many times in a career, let alone a season.

We started the match really well and were unlucky not to take the lead when Paul Rideout rattled the crossbar with a long-range volley, but we did not have to wait long for the breakthrough.

Jason Dodd took a short throw down the right and after the ball was played back to him whipped in an inch-perfect cross for the stooping Rideout to head home at the near post. It was a trademark goal for Rideout, who would score in similar style to win Everton the FA Cup many years later.

Doddsy had a great game and, having only made his debut in another 4-1 win against Queens Park Rangers at Loftus Road the week before, must have thought professional football was easy.

Liverpool came into the game unbeaten but we had only lost two of our first nine games at that point so their confidence was high, but we soon put them in their place. Rod Wallace doubled our lead before half-time with a neat finish past my future Saints team-mate Bruce Grobbelaar from inside the penalty area after Matt Le Tissier had bamboozled the Liverpool defence with a mazy run.

Liverpool could count themselves fortunate to go in at half time only two-nil down, but it was not long before Grobbelaar was picking the ball out of his net again at the start of the second half.

Le Tiss produced a lovely piece of skill to flick the ball over the head of their red-haired full-back, David Burrows, before showing a rare turn of pace and crossing for the on-rushing Wallace to half-volley past old wobbly legs.

That was the nickname Grobbelaar, a wonderful character whom I would grow to know well, earned after his goal-line antics during Liverpool's penalty shoot-out win over Roma in the 1984 European Cup Final.

Peter Beardsley pulled one back from the penalty spot to reduce the deficit after Jimmy Case had chopped down Burrows before I played a part in our fourth goal.

Jimmy, the Scouser in our ranks, knocked a free-kick out wide and I played the ball into Rideout, who laid it off to Rod. He skinned the full-back and whipped in a cross for Le Tissier, who did not score many headers, to nod into the net

Rideout also hit the base of a post, which shows how dominant we were and it was great to share such a momentous triumph with so many of the lads I had grown up with.

I had joined the club as an apprentice four years earlier, the same summer as Matt had flown over from his native Guernsey to take the first steps on his glittering career. We would go on to become life-long pals.

We also had the livewire Wallace and the goal hungry Alan Shearer in our ranks and Doddsy, who went on to become a fantastic captain, joined us from non-league Bath City a short while later.

Matt broke into the first team a good while before me and I knew from the first moment I saw him as a schoolboy he had something special. He was a genius and there is no other way to put it.

He could do anything he wanted to with the ball at his feet and even though I played against him every day in training and had an idea of what he was going to try I still could not stop him. That just goes to show how good he was.

There has been a lot of debate about him spending his whole career at Southampton and from his point of view I am surprised he never moved on and I know he certainly had opportunities to do so.

As a visiting scout or opposition manager it would have been impossible not to be impressed with his range of skills and long-range shooting and there were clubs that tried in vain to sign him such as Chelsea and Tottenham.

There is no doubt he did come close to leaving at one stage; Tottenham were his boyhood team so it must have been difficult for Matt to turn them down but he enjoyed it at Saints, knowing he was always the jewel in our crown.

He realised he was the main man for us and thrived on being the one that had the spotlight on him. I have lost count of the number of times he produced a piece of magic to win games for us.

Shearer had the same natural talent as Matt and goalscoring came easy to him so it was no surprise to see him grow up and become such a successful player, one of the greatest this country has ever produced.

To score a hat-trick on your debut as a fresh-faced 17-year-old against a team of the stature of Arsenal, with their world-famous defence of the time, is no mean feat.

It was just a shame Shearer left when he did because Matt and him would have been an awesome strike partnership for years to come.

Goalkeeper Tim Flowers and centre-back Neil 'Razor' Ruddock were players who had been bought in as signings but were young players as well. Sadly we could not keep hold of those two for the long haul either.

Flowers went to Blackburn, where alongside Shearer he helped the unfancied Lancashire club beat Manchester United to the 1995 Premier League title, and Neil had a very successful career as a top-class centre-half for Liverpool and Tottenham among others and also won a solitary England cap.

Wallace, one of three footballing brothers, played in front of me and he was unbelievable.

People often ask me who was the best player I played with or against and without hesitation I always say Matt but Wallace comes a very close second.

If someone played a pass that was in danger of going astray, he would use the electric pace he possessed to get on the end of it and make it look like a world beater.

Importantly for me as a full-back he was also prepared to come back and help out in defence, in contrast to a lot of the so-called flair players.

Wallace was so hard to play against, very small physically and quite slight in build, but as a result had a wonderful low centre of gravity coupled with a great awareness of what was going on around him.

He was as fast as an Olympic sprinter and could outrun most opposing defenders. He also had a wicked shot on him and could score goals as well, as illustrated against Liverpool.

It would have been fantastic if we had managed to keep those young players and would have been interesting to see what the club might have achieved.

I am not saying we could have won the championship but it would have been nice maybe to have sampled some cup success. I would have swapped anything for a piece of silverware to put in my cabinet.

Sadly at the time Saints were very much a selling club so we knew it would be impossible to keep the group together but it was still heart-breaking to see that dynamic young team dismantled.

Whenever players like Beckham, Gary Neville and Paul Scholes talk about that trophy-laden group of United youngsters they wax lyrical about the team spirit and camaraderie in the group and we certainly had that too.

Some of the guys moved away from home at 15 and boys like Shearer, who had come down from the north east, and Matty were put up in digs and lived with families in and around Southampton, which must have been hard for them.

Being Southampton born and bred I had the advantage of living at home and that was settling for me.

Southampton is a very friendly and welcoming place and it was never a problem us going out for a night on the town.

We did all the usual things young boys do, played a bit of snooker and a lot of the lads enjoyed a round of golf too. I used to tag along but have never been much of a golfer so was just there for the social scene.

We had a great mix of youth and experience that all good sides need, with Case, Glenn Cockerill, Russell Osman and Rideout the senior pros in the side.

I am sure when the Liverpool players looked along the line as we waited adrenaline-fuelled in the tunnel before the game we must have looked like a team of young upstarts but the older players watched our backs in those days.

People like Jimmy and Russell, in particular, acted as minders and were quick to step in if anyone tried to bully one of us youngsters or leave a foot in to try and get into our heads.

Nonetheless, for a rookie side like that to play against a team as formidable as Liverpool, who went on to finish the season as champions for a previously unprecedented 18 times, could have been intimidating, but we played without fear.

Their forward line that night was John Barnes, Ian Rush and Beardsley. They had players like Ronnie Whelan, Alan Hansen in defence and Grobbelaar in goal.

These were names I was so familiar with growing up so to be out on a pitch competing with them and beating them as convincingly as we did is something that will stick in the memory for a long time.

The win was even more special for me because even though I am a Southampton boy Liverpool were the country's most successful team when I was growing up and I had a soft spot for them.

Kenny Dalglish was my hero and he was the player I always tried to copy when I was having a kick-about in the park with my mates.

I remember as if it was yesterday the feeling of elation running through my body when the final whistle sounded.

I was only 19-years-old and had not long made my debut in the first team so I was determined to savour every second as we made our way off the pitch.

You never know what is to come in the future but it was an unbelievable moment, made all the more special because my future wife Karen was watching from the stands along with numerous friends and relatives.

Being from Southampton I always felt an extra incentive to go out and do the city proud.

When you play for the club where you were born you know what it means to the people and I was very conscious I did not want to let anybody down.

I felt a great sense of responsibility, which never left me throughout my career.

I cannot remember too much about what happened in the dressing room after the game.

Jimmy was a Liverpool legend so I am sure he was extra proud to knock them off their perch but he had a bit of a poker face, so if he was more motivated to win because it was against his old club he never showed it.

Jimmy was old school and used to have steak and chips before every game. My pre-match meal was more modest and I always stuck to beans on toast.

I have never been a drinker so the win was not toasted with a beer by me, although I am sure that would not have been the case with some of my team-mates.

Another thing I remember from the game is Liverpool played in an all-grey strip and maybe that was an omen for Manchester United a few years later when they famously changed their kit at half-time against us.

We were 3-0 up at the interval and completely dominated Sir Alex Ferguson's men, who regularly struggled against us away from home.

The second half kicked off and it took me a few minutes to realise they had changed from the grey shirts they were wearing in the first half to a blue and white version.

My initial thought was that it was a marketing ploy as United always seemed to have at least three if not four different strips in those days.

We took our foot off the gas a little in the second half and a Ryan Giggs goal made the final score 3-1.

It was only when I picked up the papers the next day I saw Ferguson had enforced the kit change after some of the players complained they were struggling to pick out the grey shirts against the crowd.

It was quite comical really and as a result the game has gone down in folklore.

Quite often if we did get a result against one of the big teams all of the media coverage was about how poor they played rather than how well we did, which frustrated us.

We regularly felt we did not get the credit we deserved but it was always satisfying to put one over the big boys in our own, cramped back yard.

The Dell was certainly worth a few points to us over the years. It was a unique ground because the supporters were so close to the pitch and the crowd was only a few feet away.

When we were on top of our game and set about the opposition that enthusiasm spread to the terraces and it became quite a daunting and intimidating place for the opposition.

Since I have retired I have spoken to a lot of ex-players and not one of them has said 'I used to like playing at The Dell.'

Mark Hughes, who had a brief spell with us in the twilight of his career, confessed to me he never used to relish coming down as an opposition player and it was an unhappy hunting ground for a lot of the big teams.

My early memories of The Dell are walking past on my way to lessons at Bellemoor School and peering through the giant gates at the main entrance hoping to catch a glimpse of my heroes, players like Kevin Keegan, Alan Ball and Mick Channon.

I have to admit it was with more than a tinge of sadness when the turnstiles stopped clicking for the last time after the club moved to St Mary's Stadium.

I understood the reasons because with all the TV money swirling around the Premier League it was difficult to compete with gates as small as ours.

I was lucky enough to have my testimonial at the old ground before we moved and that was a night that still gives me goose bumps when I think about it.

There was not an empty seat in the house as two all-star teams managed by our then-boss Graeme Souness and the great Lawrie McMenemy faced each other in my honour.

It made me very humble that the whole city I was so proud to represent had turned out.

The fact I scored a rare goal, one of the few I got in my whole life, with my less-favoured right foot, topped off what was a fantastic occasion for me and my whole family.

Goalscoring was not something I was renowned for during my professional career, which is slightly strange considering I started out as a striker.

I played up front throughout my schoolboy days and even when I first joined Saints I saw myself as a centre-forward.

I think it was only watching Matt and Shearer in training that made me realise if I wanted to make any sort of living in the game I would need to swap positions because I was certainly nowhere near as gifted as them.

I also owe a huge debt of gratitude to Chris Nicholl and Dave Merrington, part of the backroom staff who would go on to become one of my many managers, for spotting my potential as a defender.

As someone who was sent off 11 times in my professional career, it may not surprise too many people to hear I had some disciplinary problems during my early days as a striker.

I think that came into Chris and Dave's thinking; they believed my aggression would be better channelled flying into tackles instead of trying to score goals. My only competitive goal for Saints was in December 1997, almost a decade after I had made my debut so I guess you can say it was long overdue.

When asked to contribute to this book the 2-1 win against Leicester when I finally broke my duck was high on my list of favourite games.

The fact it was at The Dell and contributed to a triumphant performance made it taste even sweeter.

There was also something poetic about the moment I had dreamt about almost my whole life because it was my old mate Matty who provided the cross for me to head into the back of the net.

The only annoying thing was I did not know how to celebrate. I had run over what I would do so many times in my head but when the moment finally arrived I froze and did not know how to react.

I think in the end I just got mobbed by my team-mates, who were all in a state of shock. I still get fans coming up to me years later saying they were there the night Benali scored.

Another thing that stands out about the Liverpool encounter is in those days we used to meet up at the Southampton Park Hotel about three hours before kick-off, have a bite to eat and walk to the ground, which would never happen now.

The walk was a part of our pre-match preparation I particularly enjoyed. It was nice mixing with supporters on the way to the game and getting their perspective on what was to come.

We went on to finish seventh that season, which was the highest position of my career and the fact we did it with such a young side magnifies the achievement.

Saints have always had a proud tradition of producing their own players and continue to do so today with players like Gareth Bale and Theo Walcott the standard bearers for the modern-day academy.

Wallace's older brother Danny, who turned out for Manchester United and England, had come through the academy system and Graham Baker – another youth product – was on the bench that day against Liverpool.

We have had players like Steve Moran so the conveyor belt and that process of the club producing their own talent was already in full flow.

The Liverpool game was not the first or last time we scored four that year; we were a team that scored a lot of goals with the striking prowess we had in the team, but we also conceded a lot.

I am not sure that is a good thing as a defender but we were certainly entertaining to watch and a month later we had a 6-3 victory against Luton Town, which is very rare to get nine goals in a single game.

It must have been a great time for supporters to watch this team. Because a lot of us were so young we played with no fear and it was a case of attack, attack, attack.

We had such an attacking threat within the team we just said: 'If you score two, we will get three or four.' That mentality was even more unusual given the manager had been a successful centre-half.

As a result of that philosophy there were many games I could have chosen as the highlight of my 16-year career at Saints, but it is the Liverpool victory and all that went with it that holds a special place in my heart above all others.

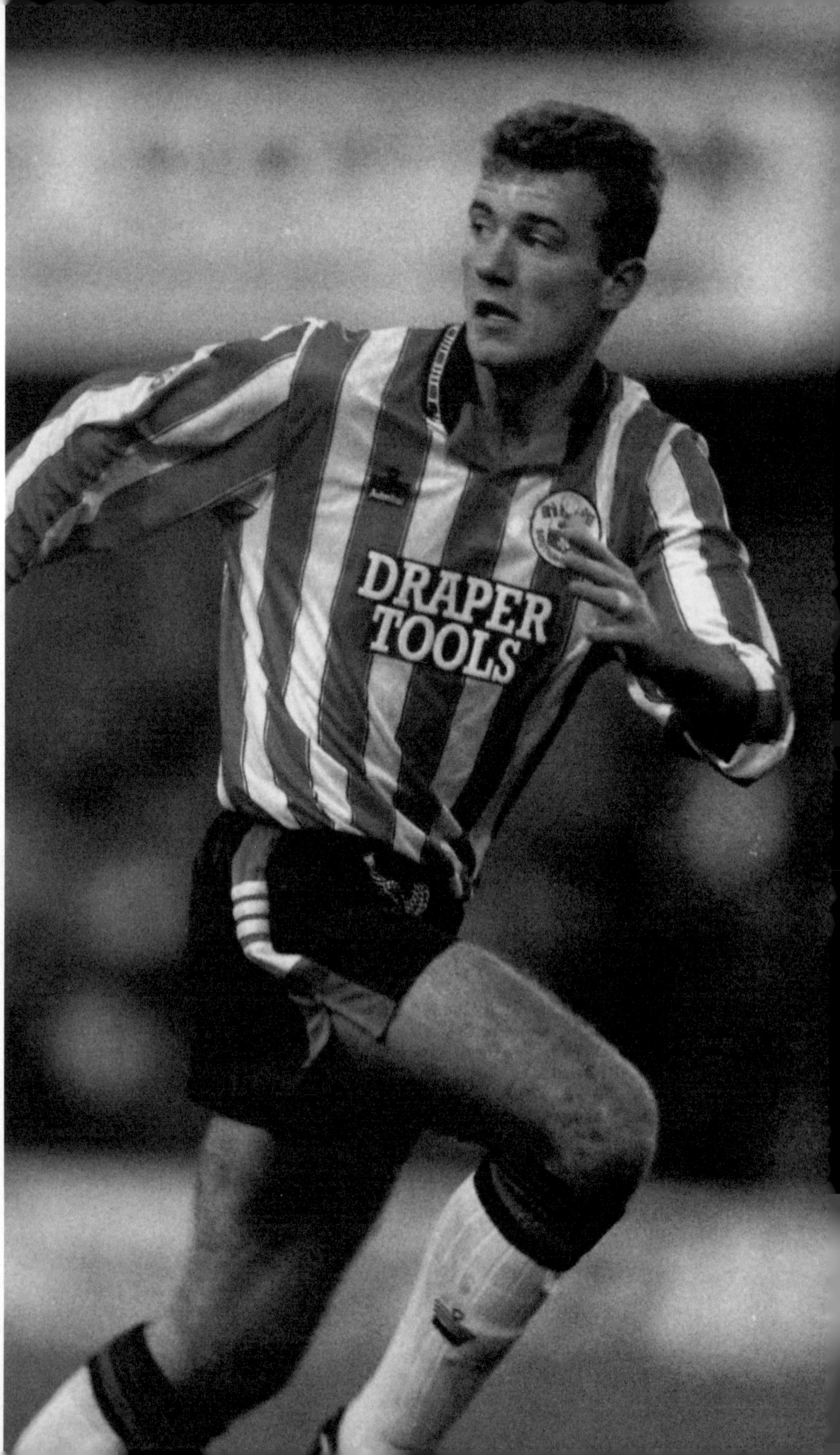
DRAPER
TOOLS

Alan Shearer

Southampton 4 (Shearer 3, Blake)

Arsenal 2 (Bond OG, Davis)

League Division One

The Dell, Saturday 9 April 1988

Southampton: Burridge, Forrest, Statham, Case, Blake, Bond, Baker, Cockerill, Clarke, Townsend, Shearer (R Wallace, 82)

'I'LL SEE you in the morning to wash all the dirty kit'. Those were the words I received from manager Chris Nicholl in the changing room after becoming the youngest ever player to score a top-flight hat-trick.

I remember the message so clearly as if it was yesterday. I guess that was his and the club's way of keeping me grounded.

After all, I had just bagged three goals in 49 minutes on my full debut against Arsenal at the tender age of 17 years and 240 days; it might have been easy to get carried away.

As it was, I would like to think it did not change me at all, I was still an apprentice on a £35-a-week contract cleaning Mark Dennis's boots, well, for a few days anyway.

I think maybe a lot of younger football fans do not associate me with Southampton and don't realise I played there but, out of all the huge choices I had to make in my career, deciding to leave the north east for the south coast aged 15 in 1986 was probably the best decision I ever made in football.

It made me grow up, made me look after myself and made me realise what I had to do to succeed in the game.

It was one of the best things I ever did although it was very difficult at the time as I had to move more than 300 miles away from home while very young.

From a footballing perspective though I have to say it was very simple.

Even growing up in Newcastle, I was aware of the history Saints had of producing players before myself and knew if I did well there I would get a chance in the first team. That was the reason I chose them.

When you see the youngsters to come out of the academy since like Theo Walcott, Gareth Bale, Alex Oxlade-Chamberlain, Adam Lallana and Luke Shaw it is clear that philosophy has not changed.

I am not surprised they are still producing talented players. What is surprising is that people have only just sat up and taken notice.

It has been going on for so many years, not just the last two or three. It was happening before my time and will continue to happen, as it is a great club.

With regards to myself, there were a couple of other offers on the table. I could have gone to West Brom or Manchester City and my hometown club were showing an interest, but Southampton just felt right.

I have always followed my gut when there is a big decision to make, whether it be turning down Sir Alex Ferguson and Manchester United or retiring from playing for England aged 30.

At Southampton we had a really good group of promising young players. The Wallace twins, Ray and Rod, were the same age as me and there was an apprentice a year older than me who went by the name of Matt Le Tissier.

It would be an ankle injury to the third and oldest Wallace sibling at the club, Danny, that would hand me my opportunity in the first XI.

The youngsters, alongside the established first team players, made it clear in my mind the club was the best place for me.

Dave Merrington helped me settle and was a friendly face as he was also from my neck of the woods. He was brilliant with all us youngsters.

I have great memories of playing in Dave's youth team and not just because of the thick wad of blonde hair I used to have in those days.

As a striker you love scoring goals and I remember hitting the back of the net most weeks in the youth side, which was obviously a great feeling.

It carried on that way for about 18 months. I must have done pretty well as I didn't have to play much reserve team football, I jumped straight up and managed to get on the bench for the first team a few times.

Being on the subs' bench straight away made me want more of the action. I made a brief appearance against Chelsea and then I got my chance. I was originally named as a substitute for the match with the Gunners but was aware Danny was struggling with a knock.

He had a fitness test before the game and I don't want to wish ill health on anyone but I really didn't want him to pass.

I knew if he wasn't fit it would open the door for me to get the nod and be in there playing. It was a great thrill to finally get the guarantee at lunchtime on the day of the game I was starting.

Despite knowing there was a chance it could happen it still caught me by surprise when, just as I had ordered a fillet steak in the canteen, the manager came in and told me three hours before kick-off.

I couldn't ever remember having a steak growing up but everyone else in the team was also down for it so I thought it was the norm.

It sounded nice anyway although I am not sure the modern day sport nutritionists all the big clubs have would approve.

The unfortunate thing about getting a last-minute call-up was that none of my family had the time to get down from up north to watch me. I was happy to have my girlfriend, and now wife, Lainya there to take it in though. I wasn't really nervous beforehand, I was just so excited, as any 17-year-old would be. I have never been one to suffer from nerves on a football pitch. I was always confident I could go and do well whoever I was up against and this was no different.

Having said that never, ever did I think I would go out and score a treble against Arsenal that day, that was a surprise and a bit of a shock.

Don't get me wrong, I wanted desperately to score and mark my big day in style but to become the youngest player ever to score a hat-trick in the first tier? That couldn't happen, could it?

The talk before the game was all about what team George Graham would put out as they were due to play Luton Town in the Littlewoods Cup Final the next week, a game they lost incidentally.

Centre-back David O'Leary was definitely out injured and his usual partner Tony Adams pulled out with the flu late on.

This meant my fellow striker Colin Clarke and I would be up against the inexperienced duo of Gus Caeser and Michael Thomas in the centre of defence. But, like I have already said, it didn't matter who I was facing, I always had confidence in my ability to go out there and do well.

You can tell how important Adams was to that side though as the only league game he missed all season resulted in me scoring three and condemning them to their biggest defeat of the campaign.

Walking out for my debut at The Dell, which as always was packed full, was a very special moment. It was one of those grounds that had so much character and atmosphere.

The supporters were right on top of the pitch and the bigger teams really did not like to come down and play there.

It took only five minutes for me to get on the scoresheet with the opener and fulfil a dream of scoring in the first division.

I was desperately trying to make an impact. As a striker a lot of it is instinct, you just do it and don't think. So many of my future goals were to come down to instinct.

Andy Townsend had done some good work in the build-up and when Graham Baker got the ball out wide, I gambled, sprinted into the box and met the cross at full speed to head past John Lukic from close range.

What a feeling. Over the years so many people have asked me what brought on the famous Alan Shearer 'hand in the air' goal celebration.

The truth is I have not got a clue. It was not pre-planned or anything, it just happened in the moment of elation and I stuck with it for the rest of my career.

We were not celebrating for long though as six minutes later Arsenal were back in the game after an own goal by Kevin Bond.

I was still enjoying myself getting into good positions in and around the box and was sure if I got another chance with my confidence sky high I could put us back in front.

That is exactly what happened when on 33 minutes I chased a ball from Glenn Cockerill and laid it off to Colin on the right wing.

He whipped a ball into the box which I managed to bravely meet in front of a cluster of defenders and head home.

We were on a high now with a real feel-good factor around the terraces and were not about to lose the lead again.

A dominant first half was complete a few minutes before the break when our young defender Mark Blake came up for a corner and powerfully shot left-footed past Lukic to give us a 3-1 advantage.

Moments after the restart Lukic initially denied me my chance to get the match ball when he made a cracking save low at my feet after I had latched on to a cross from Colin.

The partnership with Colin had clicked instantly and he would lay another ball on a plate for me seconds later, only this time I would finally put the game to bed.

His first cross was blocked but when he fired it back in again I connected with a shot I was confident would lead to another hand in the air moment.

I still had a few seconds before I could celebrate though as my effort cannoned off the underside of the bar before I could pounce on the rebound and despatch into the empty net.

At that time on the pitch I don't think I was aware I had just beaten Jimmy Greaves's record from 1960 as it had never entered my mind.

I got mobbed by my team-mates and it was all a bit of a blur. Had it all really just happened? The feeling of happiness was replaced with tiredness with about 20 minutes left to go when I was reduced to walking as my legs were absolutely shattered.

Playing first-team football compared to youth team was completely different and I could hardly walk so it was no surprise when Chris decided to bring me off.

The fans at any club always support players from their own academy and I remember getting a fantastic reception, I doubt they expected it to go so well either.

I was off the field when Arsenal mounted a late challenge and pulled one back after 82 minutes through Paul Davis, but it didn't matter as we held on for a 4-2 win.

I was ecstatic after the game more than anything, delighted it had gone so well because when you come in for people who have been doing well you don't want to let anyone down.

After Chris's wise words in the changing room there was no major booze-up with the team after the match for me. I just went out with friends for something to eat.

The match ball went straight up to the north east the following week and my mum and dad have still got it. It is one of our prized possessions.

My years as an apprentice were soon over though as the boss called me into his office a few days later and I signed my first professional contract.

I think I took everything in my stride. The only thing I would say is that the game against Arsenal got my name out.

One day I was scoring regularly in the youth team which you would only know about if you are involved inside football or a very knowledgeable fan of the club.

Then all of a sudden I scored a hat-trick at 17 and my name was on the back of newspapers and everyone knew about me. I was no longer just that guy from the youth team.

But in a way I made it difficult for myself as people expected me every single week to be banging the goals in and, of course, as I was so young I couldn't deliver.

It became quite hard. I had been out and scored three and certain people thought I could do it a lot of the time. Obviously it was not going to happen.

For the next 18 months or so I didn't hit the target very much or get many goals. I played two more games that season and failed to register a goal.

The whole of the next campaign did not go to plan either, I was by no means a first-team regular and struggled to replicate my best form. I played just eight matches the entire season, without scoring.

Southampton at the time were not one of the teams who were going to finish in the top half of the table so at times we were fighting off relegation.

For a young kid playing in that situation and under that pressure was difficult. It was important to have a good set of friends around me to help.

Neil Maddison, also from the north east, was a great pal of mine as we used to share digs together for a year or two when I first came down, before I moved in with Lainya.

I was also good mates with Le Tissier and Rod Wallace as they were around the same age as me. Those were my main mates.

Matt was an apprentice when I first joined but already by then he was a great player, absolutely fantastic.

He was only a year older than me but I still admired him for what he was and what he could do with a football at his feet.

He could do most things with a football, left foot, right foot, pass, shoot and he scored great goals. He was very calm, nothing ever affected him, and he was so laid back.

I am not one who thinks he should have moved on as he was happy with what he was doing and achieving at the club. He is to this day.

That is not me saying he could not have gone on and played at a bigger and top football club, I don't think anyone could have doubted that, but he wanted to do it his way and that probably cost him more England caps.

He was what he was. There is no doubt he had the talent to be in future international squads.

But he loved Southampton, the area, club, fans and his role in the side. He didn't want to leave and I respect that.

Things started to happen for me again in the 1990/91 season when I was voted player of the season by the fans.

I scored in my first appearance of the campaign against QPR and established myself in the first XI. I went on to play more than 40 games and score 12 league goals.

Playing as the main striker with Matt and Rod either side of me was a real handful for any defence in the league and we all got into double figures in the goals chart, playing some really good football.

This form earned me international recognition as I was picked for the England under-21 side to play the Toulon tournament in France, which we won with me getting the award for top scorer and player of the competition.

I came back hungry for more success and became more prolific under new manager Ian Branfoot in what was to be my last season at the club. I got 20 odd goals in all competitions.

We finished 16th in the league and got to the final of the Zenith Data Systems Cup, losing 3-2 in front of 67,000 fans to Brian Clough's Nottingham Forest at Wembley.

My exploits got me a call-up to represent the senior England squad where I managed to score, along with my now *Match of the Day* colleague Gary Lineker, on my debut against France.

It was a great time for me and a nice feeling to get recognition for all my efforts with Southampton that season.

Some people say you have to be playing for a fashionable club to get called up for England but if you do well enough you will get your chance, as shown by Rickie Lambert when he scored on his debut against Scotland as a Saints player.

Up until that stage there were probably not enough goals in a red and white striped shirt but 20 in that last season got me involved with the Three Lions and eventually led to a place in the squad for the 1992 European Championships in Sweden.

I wanted to go, was desperate to go. I was aware it was tight for places but I was delighted I was able to get the nod from Graham Taylor.

When back from Sweden after finishing bottom of the group, my future was in question as I was made aware there was interest from several clubs who were prepared to break the British transfer record for me.

There had been rumours throughout the season clubs such as Manchester United were going to come in for me but I was not really taking much notice.

When away at the tournament I was not thinking about my future all the time, the move all came about quite quickly.

I knew Ray Harford from the England under-21 set-up and he was at Blackburn at the time. He played a big part, along with Kenny Dalglish and Jack Walker, in talking me into going to Ewood Park.

Blackburn were set to pay £3.6 million for me but despite still being a young man I knew it would not affect me.

I was 21 when I signed but I didn't feel the pressure of the transfer fee, I loved the fact someone was prepared to pay all that money for me.

When you talk about £3.6 million nowadays it doesn't seem a lot but back then it was a hell of a lot of money.

But I always back the fact if someone is prepared to pay that for you then it is not your gamble. It gave me belief and confidence that they wanted me that much and had great belief in what I was doing.

Just as it was a huge decision to join Southampton in the first place, it was also incredibly difficult to decide whether to leave or not as I was so happy at the club.

In fact it was a massive decision. I was a young married man and my wife was eight months pregnant at the time, it was a huge call for the both of us to make.

I suppose you can say the rest is history. I went on and had a wonderful career with many special moments in the game whether it be breaking records or captaining my country.

However, I will never, ever forget that game against Arsenal. When asked to do this book it was the first game that came into my head.

I owe a hell of a lot of my career to Southampton. It was a great learning curve for me which was the reason I signed in the first place.

As I have said it was a tough call to leave home at 15 but everything I had hoped for, happened. I absolutely loved my time there.

I grew up, looked after myself and got a first-class grounding at a great football club. I learned the game and was brought up in a fantastic way by the staff there.

I have still got friends down on the south coast and visit the area on a regular basis with my wife to see her family.

The Saints result is always one of the first I look out for and it is great they have been doing so well again with all the top home-grown talent they have nurtured over recent years.

Their rise back from League One is a fantastic success story. For players like Lallana and Lambert to play in all the leagues they have with the club, it is fitting they are now getting the recognition they deserve.

With my history and connection to the club I have even been rumoured as a potential manager for them in the past, but going back into management does not interest me at the minute.

I am very happy with what I am doing. There are so many rumours in football and like my amazing debut, some things can be hard to believe.

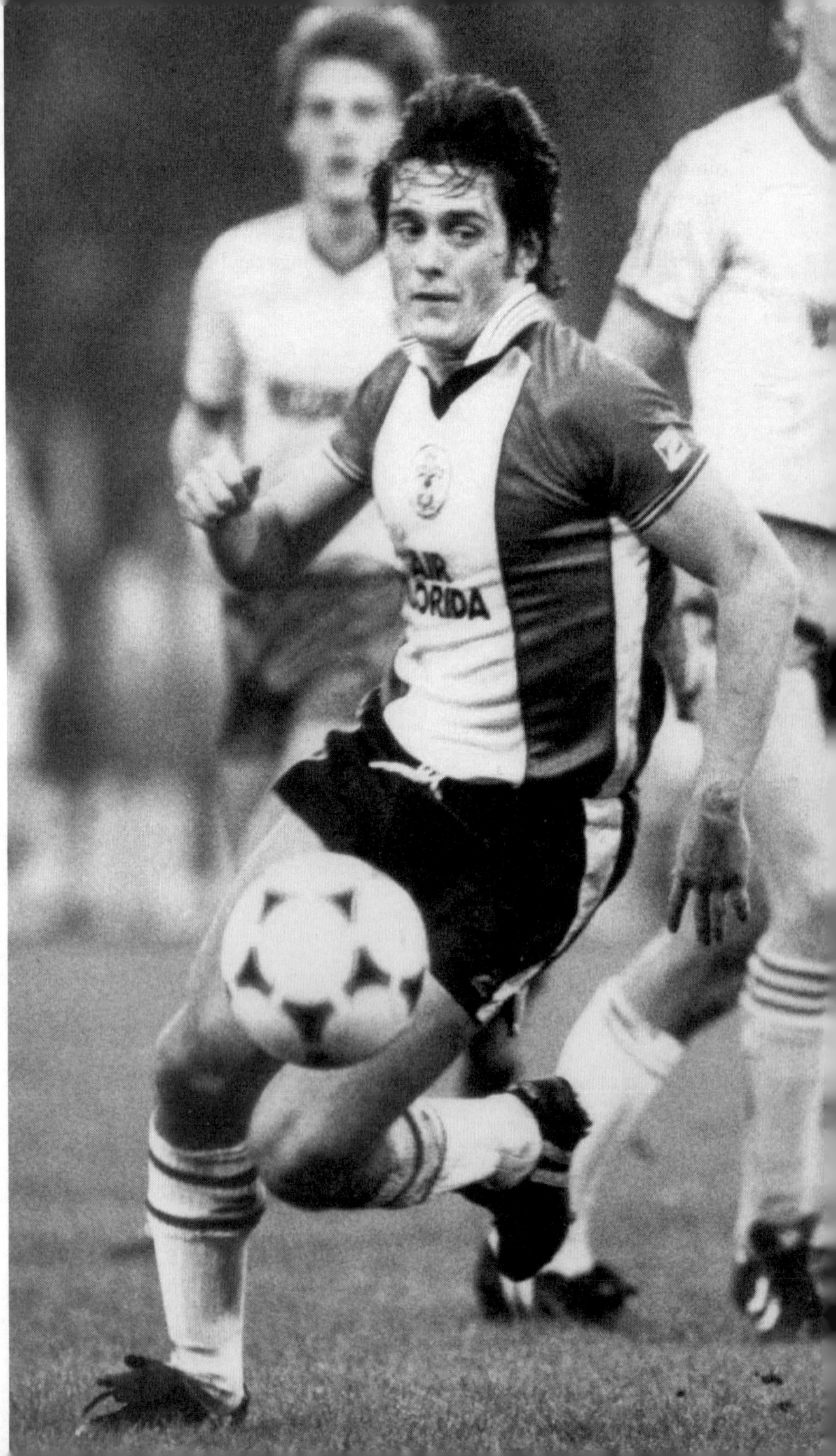

STEVE MORAN

Steve Moran

Portsmouth 0
Southampton 1 (Moran)

FA Cup 4th round
Fratton Park, Saturday 28 January 1984

Southampton: Shilton, Mills, Wright, Dennis, Agboola, Armstrong, Williams, Holmes, Worthington, Wallace, Moran

AS I stood in front of our delirious supporters with both arms raised above my head and the elation beginning to wear off, a sudden realisation dawned on me, 'What the hell have I done?'

A local lad who went to school in Fareham in a class full of Portsmouth fans had just scored a last-minute winner to help their fiercest rivals dump them out of the FA Cup in their own backyard.

If I had stuck the ball in the net a few minutes earlier, giving the 30,000 Pompey supporters longer to take in what was happening I am convinced I would have sparked a full-scale riot.

Seeing as my goal had come so close to the final whistle I made sure that once the game re-started I spent the rest of the match hovering as close to the tunnel as possible in order to make a swift exit from the pitch.

The rivalry between Southampton and Portsmouth is like no other I have experienced in my career and the atmosphere inside Fratton Park that afternoon was filled with hatred.

It was a very intimidating place to play and staring into the crowd was like looking into one big angry face. I tried not to lock eyes with any individual.

No one section of the home support was worse than the others. The grannies were just as aggressive and vitriolic as the teenagers.

There wasn't a fixture like this at the other clubs I played for during my career. At Leicester we didn't really have a local derby and Exeter against Torquay was small fry in comparison.

Hearing what other players have said, the south coast derby is as nasty as it gets.

I was a natural target having been caught up in some unsavoury, and ultimately false allegations, during an earlier pre-season tour in Sweden.

I got jip for that at every away ground we visited. It went with the territory, but I always took it as a compliment when they singled me out for verbal attention. It meant I was seen as a threat otherwise they wouldn't waste their breath.

The two clubs were in separate divisions and had not played each other since 1976, when a solitary Mick Channon goal resulted in another 1-0 Saints win which helped relegate our neighbours to Division Three.

The fact this was not a regular fixture made it all the more special and anticipated so the build-up was that much more intense, with special supplements published in the local newspapers and extra media interest.

Despite playing their football in the then-Division Two, Portsmouth were not a bad side at the time. They fancied their chances and were very bullish about it in the days leading up to the match.

It was their great chance to put one over their rivals so we just wanted to keep them down in their place and had been playing well enough that season not to think any differently.

Bobby Campbell was the home manager and they had Alan Biley and Mark Hateley up front but we were the bigger side and thought we should see them off having beaten Nottingham Forest 2-1 away from home at the City Ground in the previous round.

Our fans had been given the whole of the Milton End terrace so the atmosphere was pretty manic at our end with both sets of supporters trying to outsing each other.

We just did our usual pre-match warm-up, taking extra care to make sure we stayed in front of our own supporters.

As a player you could not help but get swept up in the intensity of the occasion but, all in all, it was a pretty disappointing game for the neutral.

Portsmouth had the better of the chances and Biley missed a glorious opportunity to send them into the next round a couple of minutes before I scored when he blazed over from close range.

I was up against Mick Tait, whom I would go on to play with at Reading when he was also my room-mate.

Tait was a renowned hard man and I expected to be kicked by him but he later admitted he couldn't get close enough to me.

He wasn't the easiest player to play against. He certainly was no holds barred but I had quite a bit of joy against him. After scoring in this game, the next time I faced him for Exeter against Darlington I scored four.

Before my goal I cannot remember us having too many openings and when I look back now the lead-up to it was all out of sync to how we usually played.

It came from a throw around the halfway line on the left-hand side.

For some reason Frank Worthington was out on the left wing and he hooked the ball with his unfavoured right foot down the right channel to Dave Armstrong.

I don't know why Dave was there because he always played on the left and had to cross with his right peg, which was just his standing foot.

My philosophy was always to get into the box as often as possible because the more you are in there the more chance you have of scoring.

The cross from Dave was really inviting and the ball ran right across the penalty spot into my path.

The way I was coming in I'd have preferred to hit it with my right foot but it was waist high so I had to open my body up and hit it with my left. I was praying for the ball to hit the target because I was aware there was not long left on the clock.

I got a good, clean connection and angled the shot down to the right hand post. Alan Knight dived that way and got a strong hand on it but not enough to stop it going in and could only push the ball into the side netting.

We realised it was in and all hell broke loose. The home end fell totally silent.

It was one of the most satisfying goals I have ever scored and the one whenever I meet Saints fans they want to talk about the most.

The amount of people who tell me they sneaked off work to go and watch the game and how much it affected their childhood because they had the bragging rights for years to come is incredible.

The only one on the same scale is the winner I scored at Anfield in the last couple of minutes against the then European champions Liverpool in 1981.

It was such a bizarre goal, with all the players being in the wrong position, that when the two teams were paired together in the FA Cup in the 1990s and we were asked by Meridian TV to recreate it in a 'Fantasy Football' style, it took us about 40 takes to get anywhere close.

I used to lose my head whenever I scored and still cannot work out how some players can execute a pre-planned goal celebration in the heat of the moment.

I would just run around like a lunatic and on this occasion headed straight towards the away end.

I got as close as the stewards would let me to the huge caged fences stopping our celebrating fans from spilling onto the pitch.

I have seen some players taunt the opposition supporters after scoring, especially if they have been taking a bit of stick but safe to say I never even considered running towards the Pompey end. I don't think I would have made it back up the M27 in one piece if I had.

I also think it is fair to say Hampshire Police shared my joy. I don't think they would have relished the prospect of a Tuesday night replay at The Dell.

As I have already mentioned, despite being born in Croydon, I grew up in Warsash and was a pupil at Prices Grammar School in Fareham.

I was always a big Southampton fan, even before joining the club, and we were the better side when I was a kid but I had a lot of mates who were mad Pompey supporters, which always sparked some good-natured banter in the playground.

I first realised how intense the rivalry was when as a Saints apprentice I decided to have a night out in Portsmouth.

I went with a few mates to a nightclub called Joannas on Southsea seafront and was recognised by a group of lads and the situation turned quite nasty.

I was confronted by one of them who was being egged on by his pals and threw a punch at me.

I left pretty rapidly but later found out my attacker was a certain David Leworthy, who was on Pompey's books at the time and came from a family renowned around the city for being pretty hard.

Frank Burrows was their manager at the time and when he found out about the incident, Dave was thrown out of the club.

He would go on to play for Tottenham and we actually ended up as team-mates at Reading, which I suppose was a little bit bizarre.

I also remember attending the derby game in 1976, hoping I didn't catch the eye of anyone I had gone to school with in case they recognised me as a Southampton player.

It wasn't a very nice atmosphere then so I guess it gave me a taste of what I could look forward to when the cup draw was made.

I don't recall too much about the morning of our game but the club made the sensible decision to leave our departure as late as possible as it was only a half-an-hour drive along the motorway.

We had a pre-match meal at the Southampton Park Hotel before getting back into our cars and driving to The Dell to board the team coach.

The traffic was pretty busy with carloads of our supporters heading in the same direction and as we got closer to Portsmouth we noticed some less than welcoming banners hanging from the bridges above the carriageway.

The extra security measures the police had imposed meant there were not too many Southampton fans to greet us as we stepped off the coach.

It parked up behind the Milton End, leaving us a short walk to the players' entrance. It was not the greatest situation to be in because there were quite a few points where we could have been ambushed by their supporters.

Not that the away dressing room was any more welcoming. Fratton Park was an old-fashioned stadium and the away changing room a dingy little place.

After the game the atmosphere around the ground was a bit more sinister because we had won and there were reports of a few of the supporters' coaches being attacked with rocks. Thankfully we managed to avoid getting caught up in that.

I always thought the hatred seemed to come a lot more from the Portsmouth side and maybe that was because of the fact at that time they were the underdogs and had been living a bit in our shadow.

Lawrie McMenemy was our boss and he was excellent at man-management so left us under no illusions as to what the game meant to our supporters.

Lawrie's victory jig on the touchline is another highlight from the win. I don't think I was looking over to him but have seen it on television. It wasn't very well coordinated.

The gaffer wasn't the most technically gifted even when he was laying balls off to us in shooting practise in training.

He always maintained he used to be testing us with some of his passes but frequently what should have been a right-foot volley ended up being a header and vice versa.

Lawrie always kept very serious about most things but the occasion must have got to him as it should do, beating our local rivals in such dramatic fashion.

He was almost like a father to me and likes to tell the story about how he bought me my first pair of decent football boots.

Lawrie was looking for a team for his son and came to watch my schoolboy team Sarisbury Sparks.

He came across this young lad slipping around with a pair of old moulded studs against a team we should have been beating 10-0.

Lawrie came and had a word with me at half-time and said 'Score me a hat-trick second half and I'll buy you a pair of boots.'

I scored the quickest hat-trick in history and he was true to his word. He took me to a local sport shop in Fareham and told me to pick whichever pair caught my eye.

When I first broke into the Saints first team he used to have a go at me because I had a tendency to put weight on quite quickly.

He could see I was a youngster and could be beneficial to the team. His way of managing me was sometimes to have a go and sometimes put an arm around my shoulder.

We had a lot of experience in the team in the likes of Worthington, Steve Williams, Danny Wallace, myself and Armstrong.

Then there was Mark Dennis, who got hit by a coin late in the game, which resulted in the stoppage time during which the throw-in leading up to my winning goal was taken.

Mark had a reputation for play acting to waste time at the end of games we were winning and would regularly go down in a heap with a mystery 'injury' when he was furthest away from the benches to use up a few valuable seconds, but his crying wolf antics worked properly this time.

Mark would have loved the atmosphere and had been winding up the Portsmouth fans every time he went over to the touchline.

He was an absolute nutter and even his team-mates didn't trust him. You didn't know what he was going to do next. One minute he would be smiling at you and the next he would head butt you.

I remember him having a fight with Peter Shilton on a pre-season tour.

Shilts was a big fella so when it spilt out into the hotel foyer and they were rolling about on the floor with our goalkeeper on top, you would have thought he had got the better of Mark. But Shilts stupidly thought it was over and got in the lift to go to his room and as the doors were closing Mark rushed in behind him to finish the job.

Mark came out on top, judging by the bruises on the two of them at breakfast the next day.

I remember another time when Mark's pit-bull terrier was wanted by the police after eating the neighbour's cat.

He was a lovely guy but you'd want him on your side because when he was off on one you would have to kill him to stop him.

As for Shilton, he was a fantastic trainer and if we were doing a shooting session, and he had his mind on the job, he was almost unbeatable.

So much so if you did score it would have to be an unbelievable strike. For me as a striker practising against him made me a better finisher.

I came up against him very early on in my career playing for Saints away at Forest when I found myself one-on-one with him after running from the halfway line and managed to go round him and slot home.

I reminded him about that a few times when he joined the club but, to be honest, he wasn't one you took the mickey out of too much, his ego was too big. He had been there and done it and liked to tell you that.

He would turn up just before training started and leave as soon as it was over. He was a total loner and was not overly popular with the other lads, or he chose not to be.

He would only mix with the senior players and was a bit of a strange one but you couldn't help but respect him because as a goalkeeper he was tremendous.

Despite the animosity on the terraces we still managed to join the Pompey lads in the players' lounge for a drink after the game.

The bar at Fratton Park was like a big house and you had to go out of the ground to get back in and as we did a fan had a pop at Steve Williams.

It all died down pretty quickly as the stewards moved in but Steve was a fairly obnoxious character himself and probably an easy target because the fans would have known they would have got a reaction. The guy did well not to pick on Mark Dennis.

Steve was a fantastic footballer, very strong in his own beliefs of what should and shouldn't be done.

Even as a youngster he didn't think twice about having a go at the senior players like Channon, Alan Ball and Kevin Keegan.

He was very outspoken and set in his ways but an excellent pro; a winner with a nasty streak in him and Lawrie loved him for that.

It didn't do us any harm in the changing room seeing somebody who would fight their corner when he thought he was right and even when he thought he wasn't.

He played for England when they beat Turkey 13-0 on aggregate, which, looking back now, was an extraordinary scoreline and, but for injuries, he would have got more caps.

My big mate in the dressing room was Nick Holmes, who was also a local Warsash lad. I played golf with him and he used to give me a lift into training.

Nick and Chris Nicholl were very close and got on well off the pitch and he kept me pretty grounded. If he thought I was doing well he would tell me and if he thought I wasn't he would be on my case.

He gave me a lot of advice, especially around the golf course when you get a bit more time than in training or after matches.

Nick was a Jekyll and Hyde type, the quietest, nicest person off the pitch but an absolute loon on it. He had white line fever and wanted to win at all costs.

I have to admit after winning this game we did start to believe our name was on the cup because we had beaten Forest and Pompey away and would go on to knock out Blackburn and Sheffield Wednesday.

We found ourselves in the semi-finals along with Plymouth, Watford and Everton and, while it would have been nice to draw one of the smaller teams in the last four, we were not scared of Everton.

At that time they were not the great side they would become a couple of years later.

In fact we were so convinced we were going to beat them we made a rubbish disco version of 'When the Saints' as our cup final song.

Lawrie's son was in a band and we went along to a recording studio. That would have been embarrassing if we had made it on to *Top of the Pops*.

In the semi-final at Highbury, Lawrie took a bit of a gamble by playing Williams when he was just coming back from injury and was not as fit as he would have liked to have been.

We played Everton in the league a few games earlier and Ivan Golac had come into midfield. Steve definitely wasn't 100 per cent but we still had too much for Everton and just couldn't stick the ball in the net. We were the better side but it wasn't to be and we lost one-nil.

I was unlucky enough to get beaten in two semi-finals, this one against Everton and against Liverpool in 1986 when Mark Wright broke his leg in a clash with Shilton. Ian Rush scored two goals at White Hart Lane but it was always going to be a tall order to beat Liverpool so Everton was the one that hurts the most.

But that defeat does not dilute the joy I felt after beating Pompey. I guess it was all the sweeter for me because I trained at Portsmouth before I went to Southampton.

When I was in the first year of secondary school our under-13s got to the final of the Hampshire Cup.

We beat Yateley Town and I came on as substitute and scored two goals to win the game.

There were a lot of scouts in attendance and our whole team was invited to go to Portsmouth to train. They were going to pick the better players to take on.

I remember going training on Thursday nights and I used to hate it. We trained in a real dingy old school gym and Ray Crawford, the former Ipswich and England striker, was the youth team manager.

I just didn't enjoy it under him so when Southampton came along and invited me to train with them they did not have to ask twice.

Suddenly I was in lovely warm changing rooms and used to be able to use the sauna after practice. It was much more to my liking.

Little did I know then I would end up coming back to haunt Portsmouth on the biggest stage of all.

NICK HOLMES

Nick Holmes

Middlesbrough 0

Southampton 1 (Keegan)

League Division One
Ayresome Park, Saturday 30 January 1982

Southampton: Katalinic, Waldron, Nicholl, Golac, Holmes, Armstrong, Baker, Ball, Hebberd, Keegan, Channon

A 1-0 win away at Middlesbrough on a windswept Saturday afternoon in January may not sound like the most glamorous game in the world, but to me it meant everything.

It was the victory that took Southampton to the summit of English football for the first and, at the time of writing, only time in our history.

Being top of the first division as it was then was an unbelievable feeling; fantastic.

If you had told me it would happen eight years earlier when we were being relegated from the top flight on the last day of the season, I would not have believed you.

The Southampton board deserve a lot of credit for standing by our manager Lawrie McMenemy after the bitter pill of dropping into the second division.

I was just a young lad starting to make my way in the game when Lawrie was appointed, playing mainly in the reserves and only made a couple of first-team appearances during his difficult first season in charge.

In many ways Lawrie had the same problems when he first arrived as David Moyes did when he went to Manchester United.

Like when Sir Alex Ferguson dropped his bombshell he was leaving Old Trafford, following Ted Bates was never going to be an easy task.

Ted was 'Mr Southampton', having served the club he loved for 36 years as a player, coach and taking over as manager from George Roughton in September 1955.

During his 18-year managerial tenure Ted had taken us from the third division into the first division for the first time and into Europe. His achievements were nothing short of remarkable.

Ted just loved the game and had no conversation other than football.

He lived and died for it and if you ever caught him outside the club you could be sure he would be talking about this game or that game or about his favourite players of the time.

Lawrie was a completely different character from Ted. He was a big, loud Geordie and had not achieved what Ted had.

Ted was very popular in the dressing room, especially with the senior players who had shared many of his successes.

As you get older you become more cynical and nobody likes change, you get used to a certain way of doing things.

In those days the reserves used a different dressing room to the first team at the training ground but we heard rumblings in the main dressing room from some of the older pros.

Terry Paine in particular had been a great servant of Ted's and all of a sudden he was getting on in life and could see the end of the line.

It just didn't work out for Lawrie in those first few months, maybe it went downhill for him after he gave me my debut against Arsenal in the March of that year!

I also came on as substitute in our penultimate game away at Burnley but was not involved when our relegation was confirmed after the last match of the season against Everton at Goodison Park, going down despite a hard-fought 3-0 win against the Toffees.

If the situation was repeated now, Lawrie would have been given the sack.

The one thing Lawrie had on his side was a board and chairman very loyal to doing the right thing. Firing managers was not in their nature.

In the early 1970s it was very rare for managers to leave their posts. We had two managers in 30 years but since the advent of the Premier League it feels like we have 30 every two years.

Not that the board were left to regret their decision to retain Lawrie's services. From 1976 to 1985 we won the FA Cup, reached the League Cup Final and various cup semi-finals, regained our top-flight status and returned to European competition.

Those nine or ten years were like a dream and Lawrie was the whole reason it happened, you cannot take that away from him.

He had this knack of attracting the best players in the country to come and play for a small provincial club.

Lawrie built side after side of older players who were the wrong side of 30 but he was shrewd enough to see they still had star quality.

He put one hell of a team together in the 1983/84 season and I don't think any other manager could have done it.

I will never forget the day we got Kevin Keegan.

It was a day off for us and I was playing squash at the time when someone leant over and said 'You have just signed Kevin Keegan.' I said 'Don't be so stupid, you are having a laugh.'

I couldn't get my head around the fact a former European Player of the Year and European Cup winner would want to come to, with due respect, a small club like Southampton.

It was only when I jumped in my car and switched the radio on and heard the announcement on the news I realised the guy was telling the truth. It was another surreal moment.

Lawrie did it all under the cover of darkness, calling a press conference at the Potters Heron Hotel in Romsey to announce a mystery new signing. Nobody present could believe it when the mop-haired Keegan strolled in.

You couldn't do that now with all the media coverage but we did not have any idea. That was the way Lawrie operated and he did a similar thing with Peter Osgood.

Lawrie was also a shrewd judge of character because you never know when you bring in a big-name player if they come with baggage, but Kevin was a delight to play with and be around. He did great for the club.

He was fantastic and, considering he was one of the best players in the world at the time, was a really ordinary fella. He had a lovely family and his wife and kids had no airs and graces at all.

Kevin had an ego of course, as all the really top-class players need. He was also super competitive and on one occasion we were playing in a five-a-side tournament in Brighton and had a few hours to kill so Chris Nicholl, Kevin and I decided to have a game of squash.

I was a pretty reasonable squash player, better than Kevin but he had a great work rate and would never give up on a point, even if it seemed lost. That was the attitude he took out onto the football field.

Watching Kevin play for the likes of Liverpool and Hamburg, I always got the impression he was a decent bloke but he was even better than that.

For example, I ran the players' club for years, organising team socials and things like that and the only time the other lads had a whip round and gave me anything to say thank-you was when Kevin was there.

I never expected or wanted anything, but he insisted on taking me down to a local jewellers and bought my wife and me a china tea set, which we still have to this day. That was typical of Kevin's kindness and generosity.

One of the other things which changed when Kevin came in was we started flying to away games.

We had never done that before but all of a sudden we were leaving Eastleigh Airport and flying off in a 20-seater plane instead of spending endless hours stuck in motorway traffic on a coach.

It was brilliant and meant we could play Newcastle at St James' Park at 3pm on a Saturday and be back home by 7.30pm. I am certain it helped keep us sharper on the pitch. We did have a couple of hairy trips though as the plane we used was just a tiny little thing, not a supersize luxury jet like the ones the modern players use and I never felt that safe on board.

One trip which should have taken 50 minutes ended up taking two hours because the winds were so strong and the plane was bobbing up and down in the sky. There were some pretty green faces on board by the time we finally came in to land.

On another occasion flying to Liverpool I remember the tannoy announcer saying we were just coming into Manchester Airport. Lawrie had to shout out to remind them we were playing Liverpool and we made a hasty detour to ensure we were at the right airport.

I am sure some of my team-mates didn't like the fact the reduced travel time also cut into their card playing as it gave them less chance to gamble.

We had some serious card sharks in our ranks, although I never partook and Chris Nicholl and I took some serious flak from the others as we used to sit playing chess or backgammon instead.

Chris was my big mate in the team and we remain close to this day. I think as a player he took a bit of bad press because he was seen as the non-glamorous member of the star-studded line-ups Lawrie assembled.

He was a solid defender, there is no denying that, but Chris was more cavalier than people realise as he showed during his time as Saints manager, although I guess he had no choice with Rod Wallace and Matt Le Tissier in the side.

I can sympathise with Chris's plight because I was really the mopping boy for the likes of Kevin, Alan Ball and Mick Channon.

They were the stars of the show and I just went about my business, getting on with my job to the best of my capabilities as I had always done.

Channon was another quality player who was also an unbelievable person, but he was the worst trainer I have ever seen in my life.

During practise games he used to stand with his arm leant against the corner flag, but come a match-day he went out and gave everything so Lawrie never took him to task over it.

He would never allow us younger players to get away with putting in less than 100 per cent in training but turned a blind eye to it for the older ones.

Lawrie was good like that and learnt to make allowances. He was shrewd enough to realise you don't coach the Keegans, Channons, Osgoods and Alan Balls of this world.

Jock Stein and Ferguson were Lawrie's big mates and I think those three were very similar in the way they ran a club.

None of them will go down as the greatest coaches in the world but their skills were in man-management and getting the best out of individuals by whatever means necessary.

The biggest strength for Kevin, Bally, Channon and Osgood, as well as their undeniable natural ability, was a will to come out victorious at all costs.

I always knew during our five-a-side games if I ended up with them on my team we would win.

They were strong characters, not afraid to speak their minds and if you were not performing to a certain level they would tell you in no uncertain terms.

I was lucky that I didn't take too many rollickings from our superstar quartet as, although I wasn't quite as gifted as them, they could see I always gave my all and that my strengths were in other ways.

My memory of some of the games I played in is not the best. You tend to remember your bad moments, like the FA Cup semi-final defeat to Everton in 1984, which still sticks in my mind as one of the low points of my career.

Looking at the Middlesbrough match, I remember it had been quite a bad winter and we were able to take advantage of playing our games when a lot of our rivals were having matches called off.

We didn't talk about the prospect of going top much in the days and hours leading up to kick-off but we all knew deep down we had a great chance of doing so and could not have got off to a better start with Kevin putting us in front after just eight minutes.

It was a goal worthy of the momentous occasion the day would become as Bally split the Middlesbrough defence with a stunning pass for Kevin to burst onto.

Kevin still had a lot of work to do and had a crowd of defenders around him and the Boro goalkeeper Jim Platt baring down on him, forcing him wide into what looked like an impossible angle to score from.

But we are not talking about any normal footballer and Kevin somehow managed to squeeze his shot inside the post before the ball trickled over the line.

Every top team needs a bit of luck along the way and we had ours when Bobby Thomson, the Boro midfielder, blazed a penalty wide after I had harshly been adjudged to have tripped Terry Cochrane in the box.

We had chances to put the game out of reach of the home side and Kevin was denied by a smart double save from Platt but the victory was built on our stubborn defence as much as our undoubted attacking qualities.

Boro, who were battling against relegation, came out firing after we scored and could have equalised when Dave Hodgson hit the bar and Cochrane was kept out by our Yugoslav keeper Ivan Katalinic.

Trevor Hebberd had an opportunity to ease our nerves towards the end but didn't take it but, thankfully, we were not made to pay for that miss as Boro failed to find a way back into the match.

I cannot explain the feeling walking into the dressing room after full-time and hearing our rivals for top spot, Manchester United and Ipswich Town, had both lost. Lawrie later claimed it was like winning the cup all over again and I echo those sentiments.

I was absolutely elated, overjoyed. Ours had been a slow climb to the top but suddenly all the hard work we had put in seemed very worthwhile.

I have mentioned quite a lot of my team-mates from this season already and it really was a lovely side to be a part of.

Bally was a great asset to us. Even though he was in his mid-30s when Lawrie signed him he could still get around the park as well as anyone and was the greatest short passer I have ever seen.

He didn't suffer fools but had a lot of time for people who put everything in and the two of us always got on well.

Lawrie also paid Middlesbrough £650,000 to sign David Armstrong, who took a bit of time to settle on the south coast but once he did became a very important part of the team.

I am sure David would not mind me saying he didn't look like a footballer and certainly doesn't now.

David wasn't the fittest player I ever played with but had this great ability to arrive in the right areas at the right time and score goals.

I am sure he took extra special satisfaction from going back to his native north east as part of a team heading to the top of the league and looking down on his old club.

I also got on well with Steve Moran, who had come through the ranks as a young lad. I tried to look after him and he was a brainy guy who had qualifications outside football.

Steve was a lovely lad who liked the amber nectar too much but was a good finisher.

As a club Southampton always seem to unearth great goalscorers. From George O'Brien and Derek Reeves to Ted MacDougall and Steve was another name to add to that prestigious list of players who knew where the net was. Sadly Steve's career was blighted by a back injury, otherwise who knows what he could have achieved?

For me personally it was just an incredible feeling to be turning out for my boyhood club alongside such quality players.

All I wanted to do when I was a kid was play for Saints, even if we had dropped down to division four it would not have mattered because they were my team.

I first started going to games with my dad Alf in 1964 and used to get frustrated because I was too short to see the action if people were standing up in front of me so dad moved our tickets so we had seats in the stand just above the players' tunnel I came to know so well.

I joined the club quite late and was 14 by the time I got put forward for Southampton School Trials.

I must have done okay because a scout named Tom Parker recommended me to Ted on the back of the trial and it all came about quickly from there.

I went to St Mary's College, which was one of the top schools in Southampton and the expectation was if you were a pupil there you went on to do your A-levels and to university.

It came as a shock to them when I told the head teacher I was leaving school at 15 to sign for Southampton but, in fairness, they could see how much I wanted it and never tried to stand in my way.

After the Middlesbrough game we stayed at the top of the table, barring one week until 3 April but a poor run at the back end of the season dashed our hopes of mounting a serious challenge for the championship.

I do not know if our rivals seriously believed we could last the distance, but when I looked around our dressing room and saw the quality we had I certainly thought we had a shout.

Any player who tells you they don't study the league table is a liar, you cannot help it, and if people like Kevin and Bally got a sniff of glory they wanted more.

One of the games that contributed to our ultimate downfall was a 5-2 defeat to Ipswich when Alan Brazil tore us apart and scored all five goals. It is no secret Brazil liked a drink but if he had been on a bender the night before that game I will be disappointed because he was unplayable.

With the side we had you would get occasion freak scorelines like that. Kevin in particular would rather win 4-3 than 1-0.

We also drew 5-5 with Coventry City and beat them 8-2 a couple of years later.

Our fans never seemed to mind if we conceded goals because it gave them great entertainment, but the truth is we let in too many goals and lost too many games to keep our title hopes alive.

Losing, like winning, becomes a habit and once you are on a bad run at the end of the season and it becomes clear you have nothing to play for that gets into your head.

We managed to find more consistency in the run-in a couple of years later to finish runners-up behind Liverpool.

Coming second that season was probably the greatest achievement of my career but nothing will beat the pride I felt travelling home from Ayresome Park on that tiny plane knowing I had helped the club I adore reach the top of the tree. Life doesn't get any better than that.

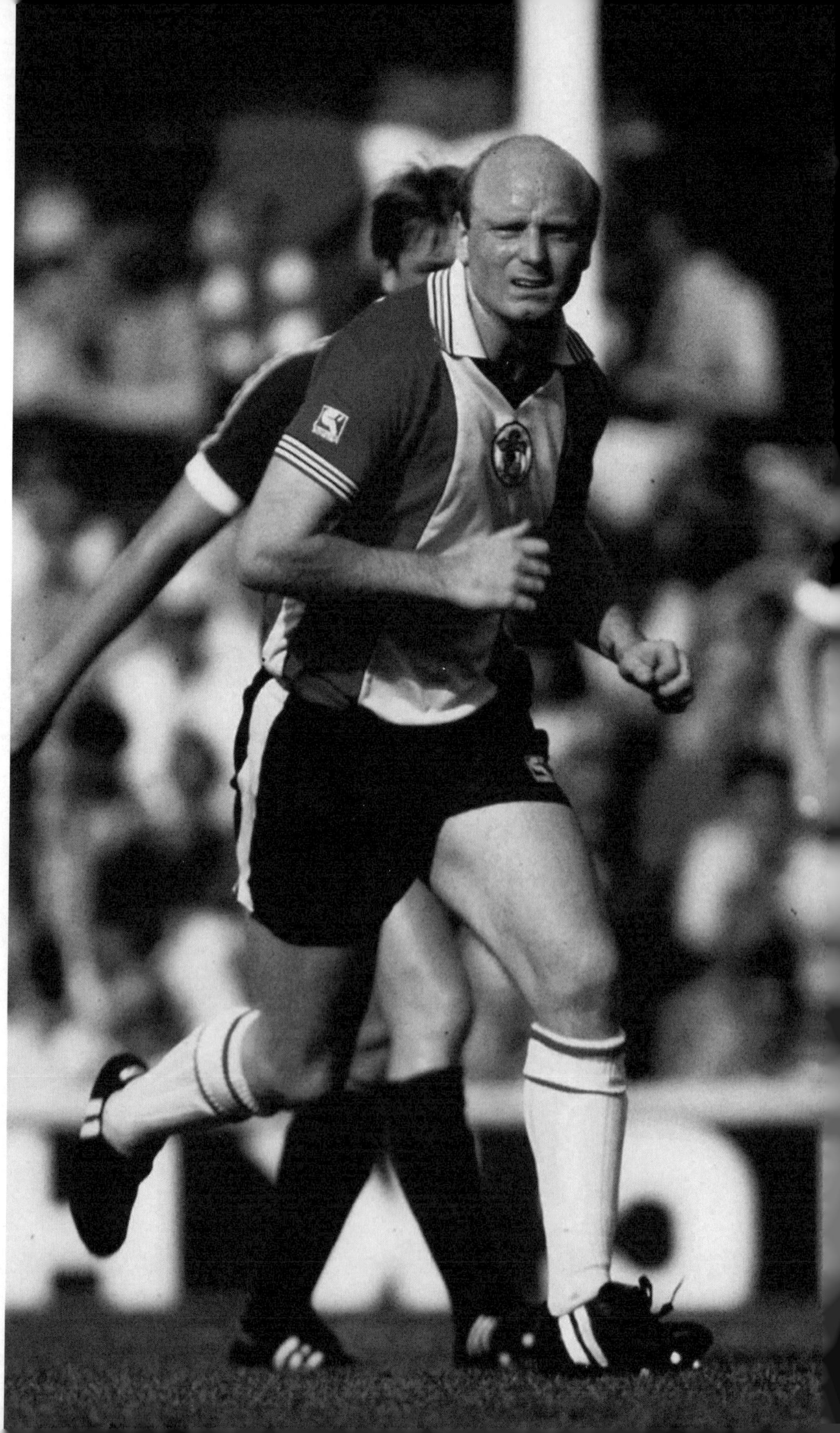

DAVID ARMSTRONG

David Armstrong

Southampton 3 (Moran, Keegan, Armstrong)

Manchester United 2 (Stapleton, Robson)

League Division One
The Dell, Saturday 5 December 1981

Southampton: Katalinic, Waldron, Nicholl, Golac, Ball, Holmes, Armstrong, Williams, Moran, Keegan, Channon

MY PAL Kevin Keegan was the country's top scorer in the 1981/82 season after finding the net 26 times but still blames me for denying him the best goal of his magnificent career. We were locked at 2-2 with United when I started a quick breakaway move with a tackle on the halfway line before spraying the ball out to Steve Williams on the right wing.

Steve chipped a pass into Mick Channon to nod it down for Alan Ball, who floated in a teasing cross and I went up and challenged Gordon McQueen, the battle-hardened Scotsman at the heart of United's defence and always a fearsome opponent.

McQueen knocked me off my feet and by the time I had picked myself up, it was just in time to see the ball nestle in the back of the net via a fantastic overhead kick from Kevin.

Kevin was at an acute angle at the time so I don't think any other player in the world would even have thought about trying what he did. I would have broken my neck had I attempted it!

It would have been one of THE great goals so we could not believe it when we realised the over-zealous linesman had put his flag up, claiming I was in an offside position when Kevin let fly.

Kevin chased the referee all the way back to the halfway line protesting the decision, and every time I see him he reminds me it was my fault the goal was not allowed to stand.

To this day I do not think I was offside. If I was, I was certainly not interfering with play so by modern rules it would never have been chalked off. Thankfully, in the last couple of minutes of a brilliant match I redeemed myself a little by ghosting in and getting the winning goal – going from villain to hero in the process.

Ironically Kevin played a big part in my goal, picking up a Bally pass down the right and jinking his way past a flat-footed McQueen before laying the ball off to Channon on the edge of United's 18-yard box.

Mickey was tackled just inside the penalty area but the ball broke kindly to me and I managed to take one touch to bring it into my stride before side-footing into the corner of the net past Gary Bailey.

It was a moment of ecstasy for everybody concerned, players and supporters alike and I ran to the crowd in complete elation.

I could see the smiles and euphoria on all the fans' faces because at The Dell you only had to walk up to the little wall behind the goal and you were engulfed by everybody.

Everyone was hugging and jumping on me and I had my arms raised aloft above my head, thinking 'what a great feeling this is'.

I had to regain my composure pretty quickly because we still had to play out added time and we knew if we could keep our concentration we had won the game.

That was the first season the Football League began awarding three points for a win so it felt even more priceless.

It was a trademark goal for me because seconds earlier I had been defending on the edge of my own penalty area and made a 70-yard run upfield, hoping something would fall for me.

To have the composure and clinical finishing I did after a long hard game was a fantastic finale to an afternoon that started badly for us when Frank Stapleton gave United the lead.

Inevitably Kevin was also heavily involved in our equalising goal, setting up his partner-in-crime Steve Moran.

Our goalkeeper Ivan Katalinic, who had become the first Yugoslav to play in the English top flight a season earlier, launched a huge punt upfield and Keegan expertly flicked the ball into the path of Moran.

Moran used his lightning pace to get in between two United defenders and buried the ball into the bottom corner from 12 yards beyond the onrushing Bailey. For our second goal Bally released Moran down the right and he raced to the byline before unselfishly pulling the ball back for Kevin to turn it home from the edge of the six-yard box.

Moran had come through the club's youth system and up until suffering a bad back injury, which knocked his confidence, was on the fringes of an England call-up.

Kevin got the best out of him and the way they played together was a real blessing. They were not the biggest strike pairing but were a handful for whoever they played against.

The understanding they had coupled with their pace and upper body strength made them a lethal combination and the goalscoring ratio they had between the two of them meant we were always going to be there or thereabouts.

At the time we played United Moran was flying, feeding off Kevin and they were great mates off the park as well.

We had a low ceiling in the home changing room and the two of them, who were each only about five foot six tall, used to have a little game and see how many times they could head the ball against the ceiling.

It meant they usually had a headache or a bad neck before we went out to play. That was a little game for them to get into the competitive spirit but Kevin usually came out on top.

They also had a competition between the two of them over the whole season whereby the person who scored the most goals got to choose where the other one took them for a meal so there was always an extra incentive for them.

They were not selfish but what it made them do was truly focus. They would not shoot selfishly and if they needed to pass they would but it made sure at least one of them would usually get on the scoresheet.

The loser used to take the winner to the Chewton Glen hotel in the New Forest for a slap-up meal.

Bryan Robson, later to be nicknamed 'Captain Marvel' by the Old Trafford faithful, got the visitors' second goal but I would go on to have the last word.

I made a rule never to worry much about the opposition because if you do you are beaten before you step onto the pitch but I do remember United that day had the likes of Robson, Ray Wilkins and Stapleton.

Because of the history and tradition of United every game they play is a cup final. Wherever they go, be it a third division club in the FA Cup or Manchester City at home, everybody wants to beat them.

The amount of success they have had over the years meant that if you played well against United people would sit up and take notice of you. Not that the players we had in our ranks were short of attention.

The way we played the game was a pleasure to be a part of. I felt that as a player, so can only imagine what our fans felt about it.

I believe we played in the right way by expressing ourselves, showing people how good we were and sending those on the terraces home with a smile on their faces.

We did that every single week at The Dell, which is why everyone associated with the club has got such fond memories of this particular era.

The whole atmosphere and aura around Kevin was electric and that brought the best out of the rest of the players.

He was so dedicated to the game but because of his ethics about how to treat people, fans, opposition players and the general public, he has been a great ambassador for the game with the way he conducted himself both on and off the field.

I cannot praise him enough. For such an iconic figure he would always spend time with everybody. He could not do enough to try to help people. He was fantastic.

Kevin was so down to earth and that is something you don't see much of in the modern game. People of a similar stature in the Premier League era appear to be aloof, but he was not like that at all.

There was nothing flamboyant about him but as a player you could not help but get caught up in all the hype surrounding him.

It was a shame he only stayed a couple of years, and the season after he left us to join his beloved Newcastle we finished runners-up so just think what could have happened if he had stayed!

Kevin definitely took that into his management career and the euphoria around him remained whether he was in charge of Manchester City or Newcastle United.

When he left us it was because Kevin felt he needed to go to a bigger club than Southampton having enjoyed success at a so-called provincial club. He was crowned PFA Player of the Year at the end of the 81/82 season.

For me, he and Lawrie McMenemy changed the whole outlook of the club and it has remained a high-profile club and stayed there ever since. Without Lawrie that would not have happened.

He had that knack of attracting the big names, experienced players who had been there, seen it and done it all at the highest level.

Lawrie has been great for Southampton Football Club and he was by far the best man-manager I played under in my career.

He had a tough job man-managing all those individuals but was the master at managing big egos and strong-willed players of different temperaments.

He would also help you deal with any personal problems you may be having to make sure your mind was totally clear to fully focus on football.

To get a coup like Kevin, twice European Footballer of the Year at Hamburg, to sign for Southampton was incredible.

The whole atmosphere of the club meant as players we could not wait for the next game to come along.

We all knew how to play and as soon as we got on the park everything fell into place. Training was short and sharp. We really dealt in quality rather than quantity. That was how we conducted ourselves and we were proud to represent the club.

We actually topped the league for more than two months after climbing to the summit at the end of January but fell away at the end, when Kevin was hampered by a back injury, and finished seventh after winning only two of our last nine games.

That was enough to clinch a place in Europe. Coupled with having big names like Keegan, Channon and Ball, who I had played against and watched play for England, and the nucleus of young players coming through, meant it was a good time to join Southampton.

I like to think I played a vital role in the whole set-up to help take the club forward.

My background was a level of consistency at the highest level and by being able to maintain that consistency we were challenging for cups and league titles. That is what I built my personal profession on.

I came in the summer of 1981, a season after Kevin had been signed under the cover of darkness. The big draw for me was the way the team played.

If you can make people, whether it be the fans, your friends or your family, all proud of the way you are playing that is what being a footballer is all about. It was a good yardstick of what we were trying to achieve that we regularly put one over the big teams.

The Dell was special because the fans were tight on you so you felt a part of them and them a part of you because they were vital to our successes and failures.

We were particularly good at home where the crowd was our 12th man. We felt like we were a goal up before we even started and walked out down those steps 12 feet tall.

We could not wait to step into the daylight with our chests puffed out and the band playing 'When the Saints go marching in' just to give us that extra boost before kick-off.

I remember before the game Lawrie went round and spoke to each individual, as he did every week, making sure they were clear on what was expected of them and what he would like them to do.

He wanted to make sure everyone who was playing was confident of what they had to do.

He kept it simple. He would reiterate just how much the club means to everybody and what an opportunity it is to make an impact at the top level. That is what we did and did it very well.

I had a very close-knit family and close group of friends so I did not socialise much with the other players but people like Channon, Kevin and Bally would go horse racing.

That was their interest outside football and Lawrie always made allowances for it as long as we were performing on the pitch.

I am sure if our standards dropped he would have made sure that if there was racing on at Fontwell he would have called an afternoon training session to make a point but he never had to worry about that.

Bally had captained Saints to promotion to the first division a couple of seasons earlier and was a true example of how professional players should conduct themselves.

In training he and Kevin would be up the front whether it be an eight-mile run or a 100-yard dash. They would want to make sure they would finish first.

I could reel off the names of all my team-mates and each and every one of them went about their business in a top quality way. High standards were expected and upheld.

Channon was more laid back in every respect, but on the pitch was a real winner and a fantastic player. He has followed that on to become a successful horse-racing trainer.

His pre-match preparation was watching the races in the players' lounge. We would come back from the hotel and he would get changed and go up there and pootle down at about quarter to three just ready for Lawrie's team-talks. I don't know whether he would listen to them or not.

As well as the standout players we had a good mix of characters in the team. Steve Williams was very strong willed and didn't take any prisoners. Even in training he would have robbed his own granny to come out on top.

Williams was a really tough competitor; a winner in every aspect.

We also had the loveable Ivan Golac, who didn't particularly like training. If he could avoid it, he would but in matches he loved to get forward, to have the ball at his feet and play little one-twos, especially at The Dell when the crowd was urging him on. He struggled to get back defensively now and again but was a real character in every respect.

He really appreciated the amount of good players he had around him and it encouraged him to go forward and be part of our build-up play.

I know it used to annoy Chris Nicholl, who was a stickler for defending and was forever shouting for Ivan to get back. We all tried to fill in the gaps Ivan would leave to make sure the team kept our shape.

To play in the manner we did, we had to have a great team ethic with strong individuals in order to make sure if the opposition caused us problems we had a good work ethic to combat them.

We played a 4-3-3 formation with me on the left wing and Nick Holmes behind me.

Nick was a quiet man but really fit and a very experienced player who knew the game inside out. We were a good unit down that left-hand side.

I was a box-to-box player, with Bally and Williams as the playmakers. The way they spread the play allowed me to get into good positions to either create goals or score goals and that was my forte, getting into the opposition box as often as possible in between doing my defensive duty.

I was never the quickest of players but I had a good engine on me and was a good reader of the game.

Whenever we went away in pre-season we were like the Harlem Globetrotters of the footballing world because of the superstar names we had.

Because of the likes of Keegan, Channon and Bally we were in demand and Lawrie liked a little trip away as well so we were always going somewhere, even mid-season we would go off to play in the Middle East.

There were lots of good sides around at that time, with Liverpool, Tottenham and Arsenal all contesting the title.

Aston Villa were crowned European champions that season so all our encounters against the top teams were really tough, quality games and the sort of matches quality players like to test themselves against the best. That is what we were doing.

Ipswich were coming to the fore under Bobby Robson and I would say each and every one of the top eight to ten sides could have fancied their chances of winning the league.

The standard in the top flight then was very high and you only had small squads. I averaged 40 games a season and would not have been happy with squad rotation even if the option was there.

United and Liverpool in particular were renowned during that period for scoring late goals so it was nice to give them a taste of their own medicine and every Saints fan remembers that moment.

I firmly believed games like this and the way we played are the reason people like Alan Shearer came down from Newcastle to sign for Southampton and Matt Le Tissier came over from the Channel Islands to play for the club.

What it did was make sure we had the continued turnover of high-calibre players coming through the system because they wanted to be involved with a club who entertained and played good attacking, attractive football.

Keegan's 'goal' epitomised that. If only it had been allowed to stand.

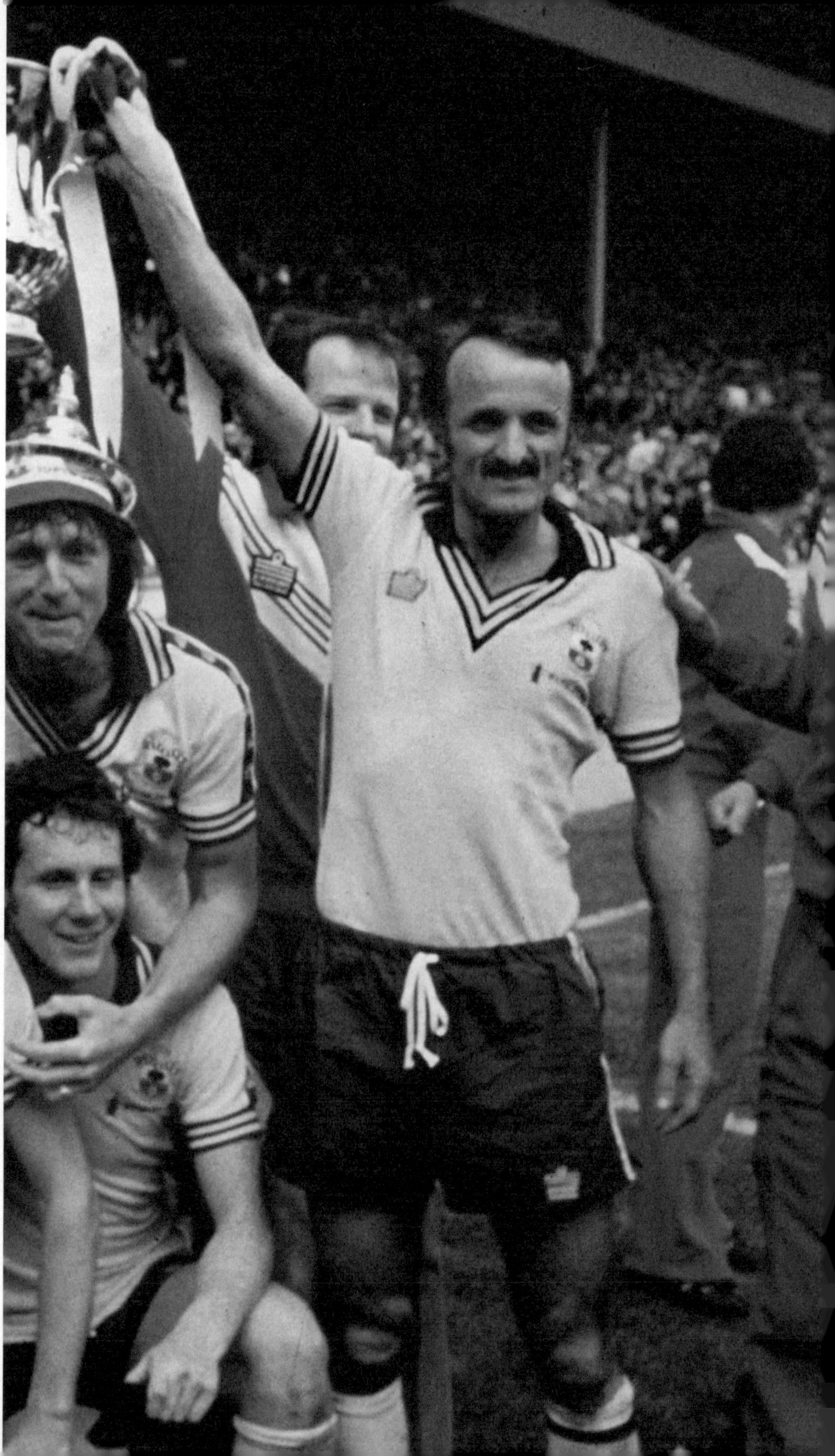

Peter Rodrigues

Southampton 1 (Stokes)
Manchester United 0

FA Cup Final
Wembley, Saturday 1 May 1976

Southampton: Turner, Rodrigues, Peach, Holmes, Blyth, Steele, Gilchrist, Channon, Osgood, McCalliog, Stokes

THERE HAVE been a lot of movies based around football but if I tried to sell my FA Cup fairy story to a Hollywood director they would tear up the script for being too far-fetched.

People still stop me in the street on a daily basis to talk to me about the events of 1 May 1976, but what they don't realise is how close I came to watching the game pulling pints behind a bar instead of walking up those famous Wembley steps to lift the trophy.

The summer before our Twin Towers triumph I had been given a free transfer by Sheffield Wednesday, which you think is the end of your career.

I was 32 so I started to look for an alternative job. I fancied running a pub, as most ex-players did in those days, and had started to contact a few local breweries until a chance conversation changed my life forever.

It all started when I was chatting to a lad called Fred Scott, a scout at Hillsborough and a Geordie like Lawrie McMenemy.

Lawrie called Fred and asked if he knew of any available players for the new season and he told him about my situation.

I came down to the south coast and met Lawrie who explained Steve Mills had been injured in a car crash.

He said he was willing to offer me a two-year contract on the proviso that once Steve was fit within five or six games I would have to drop into the reserves. I jumped at it because I just wanted to keep playing.

Unfortunately Steve didn't make it back to full fitness and then a few months later Mick Channon gave up the captaincy after a row with Lawrie so I became skipper and the rest is history.

It was fate and as I was coming off the pitch on cup final day, the cameras panned down on me and the commentator said 'A year ago he was on the scrapheap and here he is going up the steps to collect the trophy.' You couldn't have made it up.

I still remember every little detail about the day vividly. The walk from the dressing rooms onto the pitch was horrendous and that giant tunnel seemed to go on forever.

The roar from the crowd as you emerged onto the lush green playing surface lifted you and you immediately felt ten feet tall.

I was nervous but being a regular for Wales and having played in the cup final for Leicester seven years earlier, when we lost 1-0 to Manchester City, I felt in control of my emotions.

I went up to toss the coin with the United skipper and looked at Martin Buchan, who was an experienced Scotland international, and his legs were like jelly. I turned and shouted to Peter Osgood 'Ossie, he is shaking like a leaf.'

It was the same story at the team hotels on the morning of the match.

We had all the usual TV cameras in the lobby before we departed with all the lads lined up in their cup final suits and we were having a lot of banter with each other, enjoying being in the spotlight.

Barry Davies was doing the interviews and the Man United lot were at their hotel, sat outside on benches for a team photo and they looked really nervous compared to us.

As an unfancied second division team playing against one of the biggest clubs in England, we had nothing to lose and you could tell the men from Old Trafford were feeling the pressure under the weight of expectation on their shoulders.

We got to the ground about an hour and a half before kick-off. Traffic going across London was good and as we got closer to the famous old stadium we started seeing people with Saints scarves and I remember thinking to myself, 'This is game on.'

We could have been forgiven for thinking it was not our day when a United supporter stepped off the pavement into the path of the coach and we hit him.

All the lads were concerned, looking out of the bus and as we pulled into the main entrance under Wembley Way, Lawrie went out and checked he was okay and relayed that to us in the dressing room, which calmed us all down.

We came out onto the pitch all looking a million dollars in our specially-made suits with our big collars and big ties.

I spotted my daughters Amanda and Tanya, who were eight or nine at the time, up in the stands and beckoned them to come down, which was a lovely pre-match moment for me.

We had been up to look at Wembley the previous day and the United players were there at the same time as us. I called my team-mate Jim McCalliog over and told him I thought the grass was a bit too long.

Somebody from the press must have overheard as my comment hit the newspapers the following morning.

Bobby Charlton was asked about it in a TV interview and said, 'If the Southampton players are complaining the grass is long they should play on their pitch at The Dell because that has no grass at all.'

He then added: 'Besides which I think it will be 6-0 today.' I guess Bobby was not as good at seeing into the future as he was at striking a ball from 30 yards.

In any case when we got to the game the FA had cut the grass and it was in perfect condition.

Once we were inside the dressing room I went through my normal pre-match routine. I always took an hour to get changed into my kit, putting on my boots and strip in a certain order.

I looked around the dressing room and there was Jim Steele, large as life, McCalliog, sat quietly in the corner, Micky Channon with his head in the racing section of the papers, Ossie bouncing up and down and David Peach being a little bit gobby. We had a good mixture of everything.

Lawrie was a good man-manager too and was cool and collected as always.

Ted Bates had been deployed to scout the United players for us and ran through their line-up and the jobs we had to do. My job was to stop Gordon Hill and Peachy's to stop Steve Coppell. Easier said than done as they were two of the finest wingers in England at the time.

Lawrie warned us that in the first 20 minutes United would be all over us, which they were and our goalkeeper Ian Turner made a good save from Hill after having a couple of nervy moments early on.

Once we got past that 20-minute mark I thought to myself, 'We are gonna win this.' They had a load of youngsters and we had a good mixture of youth and experience, which won us the day.

Channon had a decent chance when he went one-on-one with Alex Stepney but the European Cup winner saved the shot with his legs, Ossie had a good crack at goal and even I raced to the edge of the box and ballooned an effort towards the corner flag. It missed by a mile.

I also got a whack from behind and went down. My mum was watching on TV and as they were using the magic sponge on me the water was running from my head and she thought I was bleeding.

There is a picture of Sammy McIlroy heading the ball and it hitting the top of the crossbar. I was there on the line and as I jumped up to try and clear the ball I head-butted the post.

Hill was taken off with 24 minutes to go and I stuck my feathers out and did a little strut. I felt like I had contained him and done my job.

The game went on and Channon and Bobby Stokes had gone close to scoring when eventually Bobby bagged the winner at the end of a move with only four touches.

Turner kicked the ball out, Channon knocked it in to McCalliog, who played it over the top of the United defence and Stokes put it in with a lovely left-foot finish from the edge of the box, which gave Stepney no chance. Bobby was a lovely lad. He was a gentleman. Sadly he could not handle the success and the fame that goal bought him and his career never really took off as it should have.

He was one of the best strikers of the ball at the club, a good player and a nice person. He was just a regular guy and didn't like being thrust in front of the camera for interviews.

We were in a yellow and blue strip like the Brazilians and whenever they score you see somebody flying in off camera and jumping on top of the celebrations.

I have always wanted to do that so I sprinted 40 yards and piled on top of the lads. There is famous photo which has all ten outfield players celebrating.

It was brilliant until I settled down, looked back and realised I had another 40 yards to get back. A man of my age shouldn't have done that.

For the last ten minutes the excitement got me through and I kept looking up to the Royal Box and seeing the cup like a tiny dot on the horizon. The next thing I knew I was walking up those 107 steps to collect it from the Queen.

That was the last time Her Majesty presented it at the old Wembley so that was a very proud occasion. She did not have much to say to me, just 'Congratulations, well done, did you enjoy it?' I said 'Yes Ma'am.'

I was interviewed at a supporters' club meeting some years later and the interviewer put it to me that collecting the cup from the Queen was the greatest moment of my life. But I said collecting it from the Queen, turning it half a metre and showing it off to 35,000 Southampton supporters was the greatest moment of my life.

At the end of the game I jumped up and went down on my knees. I was shaking like Buchan was beforehand. Everybody went ballistic.

After we had been up to collect the trophy we spent 20 minutes on the pitch parading it to our fans, stopping to pose for photographs in each corner of the ground.

I came down the steps carrying the cup like it was a new-born baby, staring at it and not wanting to let go. I think I managed to keep hold of it until we got to the second corner on our lap of honour.

I glanced out of my eye and saw a lot of red tracksuits as all the coaching staff and the physios joined the celebrations and it was brilliant they were in among it and as excited as we were.

I remember as a kid watching the television every year and seeing the winning captain go up to lift the FA Cup, thinking 'Wow. I wish that could be me one day.'

There was one photograph in particular I used to look at in one of the weekly magazines my mum and dad used to buy me. It was of the skipper of the amateur team Bishop Auckland sat on his team-mate's shoulders, holding aloft the FA Amateur Cup.

Then all of a sudden I was there with the FA Cup in front of me, down on the pitch and Don Taylor, the Saints physio, grabbed me and lifted me above his head onto his shoulders. It was like I had been transported onto the pages of the magazine. What a wonderful moment.

I was thinking 'This is it,' the picture of all time of me surrounded by my team-mates parading the big-eared cup around Wembley. It was like nothing I had ever experienced before or in the many years since.

The United players were upset because they were expected to win but they were gracious losers.

I got a lovely picture given to me by a photographer of me holding the cup and Tommy Docherty in the background looking dejected. It captured the moment perfectly. In fairness to him Tommy came down to our 20th anniversary bash and he spoke glowingly about Southampton as a family club. There was a nice bit of affinity with him and Lawrie.

'The Doc' had tried to sign me for Chelsea ten years before so again fate played a hand.

We had spent the week preparing for the game down at the Selsdon Park Hotel in Surrey where we took it nice and easy; relaxing, posing for pictures for the photographers and playing five-a-side matches.

I roomed with Channon and we used to watch *Little House on the Prairie* every afternoon and both end up in tears.

Lunch was always served at noon and we used to come down five minutes late so we didn't miss the end.

Apart from anything else the biggest strength of our team was we were all buddies. We were like a little close-knit community.

McCalliog didn't drink until the last three years of his career but made up for it after that. Steeley and Osgood liked a few.

We were not banned from drinking the night before the cup final so we ordered things like melon with port in and steak in a red wine sauce and sherry trifle.

It was more of a psychological thing than anything else and if Lawrie had tried to lock those lads up it would have been a disaster.

The game was played at its traditional kick-off time of 3pm on a Saturday afternoon and on the Thursday before we finished our meal Lawrie said we could have half a lager.

That cheered us up no end and was another example of his man-management skills. He knew how to handle us. Not that we ever used to take advantage of course.

Before our semi-final against Crystal Palace, Lawrie had taken the team to stay at Frinton-on-Sea in Essex to help us relax.

The town was full of old-age pensioners and there was not a bar or nightclub in sight so McCalliog and Steeley suggested we go out for a walk and try to find a game of darts.

We stumbled across a pub, only planned to have a small drink but the next thing I can remember is standing doing a crossword on the back of a six-foot door nursing half a lager and a jam jar.

We got back to the hotel just past the curfew Lawrie had imposed and we could hear the coaches talking in the background. We made a quick dash up the stairs and thought we had got away with it until we woke up in the morning and were told to get our club kit on and walk across the road to the water's edge.

Lawrie said, 'If we lose the game I am going to blame, you, you and you for being out late,' and pointed to Steeley, McCalliog and me.

I bowed my head in shame but unfortunately Ted Bates said something and Steeley and McCalliog reared up.

I said, 'Jim shut up. We were out of order.' We played the game and won and as we were coming off at full-time the cameraman filmed me walking towards Lawrie and you could lip read me saying 'What were you worried about boss?' We had a big hug and off we went.

On the night of the final and after we finally bid goodbye to Wembley we headed off to Talk of the Town, the popular nightclub that used to be on the corner of Leicester Square, had a meal and watched the live stage show they put on every weekend.

Our celebrations were interrupted at 1am when we got called back to the team hotel because the TV companies wanted to interview us while we were reading the Sunday papers.

I remember thinking it was too early to turn in for the night having just won the cup.

I later discovered Ossie, Steele and McCalliog went off to the playboy club. I wish I had known at the time because I would loved to have carried on partying the night away.

We left the capital to return to Southampton the following day. The cup was given to me so I put it on the table at the front of the coach and stared at it all the way home.

Lawrie promised we would go into the local Ford motor factory in Eastleigh win, lose or draw, to say 'hi' to the workers.

As we pulled into the factory I was still at the front of the bus with the cup, the cameras were flashing. I opened the door and the cup went missing for half an hour.

I remember as we approached Eastleigh fans were up on the motorway bridges on the M27 which were covered in red and white bunting. It took my breath away.

Then we headed off for an open-top bus ride around the city and it took three hours to get round the route because there were 250,000 people dotted around. I did not recognise any of the roads with so many people there.

I looked down from the top of the bus and there were 60 and 70-year-old guys in tears and it dawned on me we had done something for them and for the city.

At the end of the parade we arrived at the civic centre for a special mayoral reception. Someone in the crowd had given me a hat to wear so I put in on. I was ready to greet the Lady Mayoress and forgot to take the hat off until one of the lads reminded me just in the nick of time.

We came out onto the balcony at Southampton Guildhall and had a sing-song with the crowd. There were thousands of people there and ship hooters sounding all around. The city was totally alive.

A week later we had to go back down to the civic centre to replace all the roses that had been trampled on by supporters.

In those days I only lived four minutes' walk from The Dell and my neighbours were nice people but very unassuming.

I couldn't believe it when I turned into my road and they had decorated the front of my house from top to bottom in red and white bunting by way of congratulating me.

I was still buzzing and there was no way I was going to sleep with all the events of the last 24 hours still racing through my mind so I decided to carry on drinking at my local pub the Clump Inn.

It was quiet as it was a Sunday and there were only a few people there. As I walked in the landlady, Barbie Cotterill, started screaming and said she could not believe I had chosen to go there after winning the cup.

She said it was her wedding anniversary. I had a nice evening with Barbie and her husband Pete, toasting their and my big day.

The following Monday the whole team headed off to Newbury racecourse to continue the celebrations. Ossie was a racing man and he took a fiver off each of us to put on a horse.

I glanced at the race card and there was a horse called 'Our Anniversary' so I asked him to put my fiver on that because of the conversation I'd had the previous night. There were three furlongs to go and the horses were galloping down when suddenly Our Anniversary came storming up the rails and romped home at 20-1.

I said, 'Ossie, you owe me a hundred quid.' He stared at me blankly as he had forgotten to put the bet on and I never got my money.

Ossie was a top man. My fondest memory is of him standing in a corner of a bar, with a large glass of Chardonnay in hand holding court with his mates.

He would always try and keep the team together and we all used to visit him in a little pub in Bishop's Waltham where he hung out.

We were lucky to still be in the cup at all when we drew 1-1 with Aston Villa in one of the early rounds.

We were 1-0 down in the 89th minute on a windy, grotty day at The Dell when Hughie Fisher came to the edge of the box, swung his left foot at the ball and it flew into the back of the net. People have since said it was Hughie's greatest moment as a Saints player.

Then we played them in a replay at Villa Park, the match went to extra time and we beat them 2-1.

We also played West Brom and on the day of the game, Channon, Bobby Stokes and a few other players went down with a sickness bug.

We had to dig deep to nick another 1-1 draw, got them back to our place on a Tuesday night and were 4-0 up in minutes and got through that tie quite easily.

Then we played Bradford, who could have been a bit of a banana skin for us as a third division side but we snuck through that one on a bad pitch thanks to Peter Osgood's volleyed goal.

We would have chosen Palace, managed by the flamboyant cigar-smoking Malcolm Allison, as our semi-final opponent and we beat them comfortably 2-0 at Stamford Bridge.

Then all of a sudden you realise that you are at Wembley.

The following Monday I sat in the old ITV studios in Southampton, looked out of the window and there were some gas towers in the background. I said to the presenter, 'They look like the twin towers to me.'

I watched United's 2-0 semi-final win over Derby on TV and they looked awesome; Hill and Coppell in particular were unplayable.

Docherty went on to say 'This was our cup final.' I guess 'The Doc' got that wrong too.

The other standout memory of the whole occasion is of the wife of a pal of mine promising to give me a striptease if I touched my nose as we walked out of the tunnel.

We were due to holiday in the south of France that summer, my friend and his wife and my wife and I. She said if I gave her the secret sign I would be treated to a full frontal.

I agreed and as I came out of the tunnel with the match-ball under my left arm, on what is the greatest day of my life, that was all I could think about.

I scratched my nose and reporters were onto it like a ton of bricks, asking why I did it and I have never revealed it until now.

Off we went on holiday to St Tropez. The lady's husband beckoned me into the shower and out she jumped shouting 'there you are Rodrigues' with her top off.

Who says FA Cup dreams don't come true?

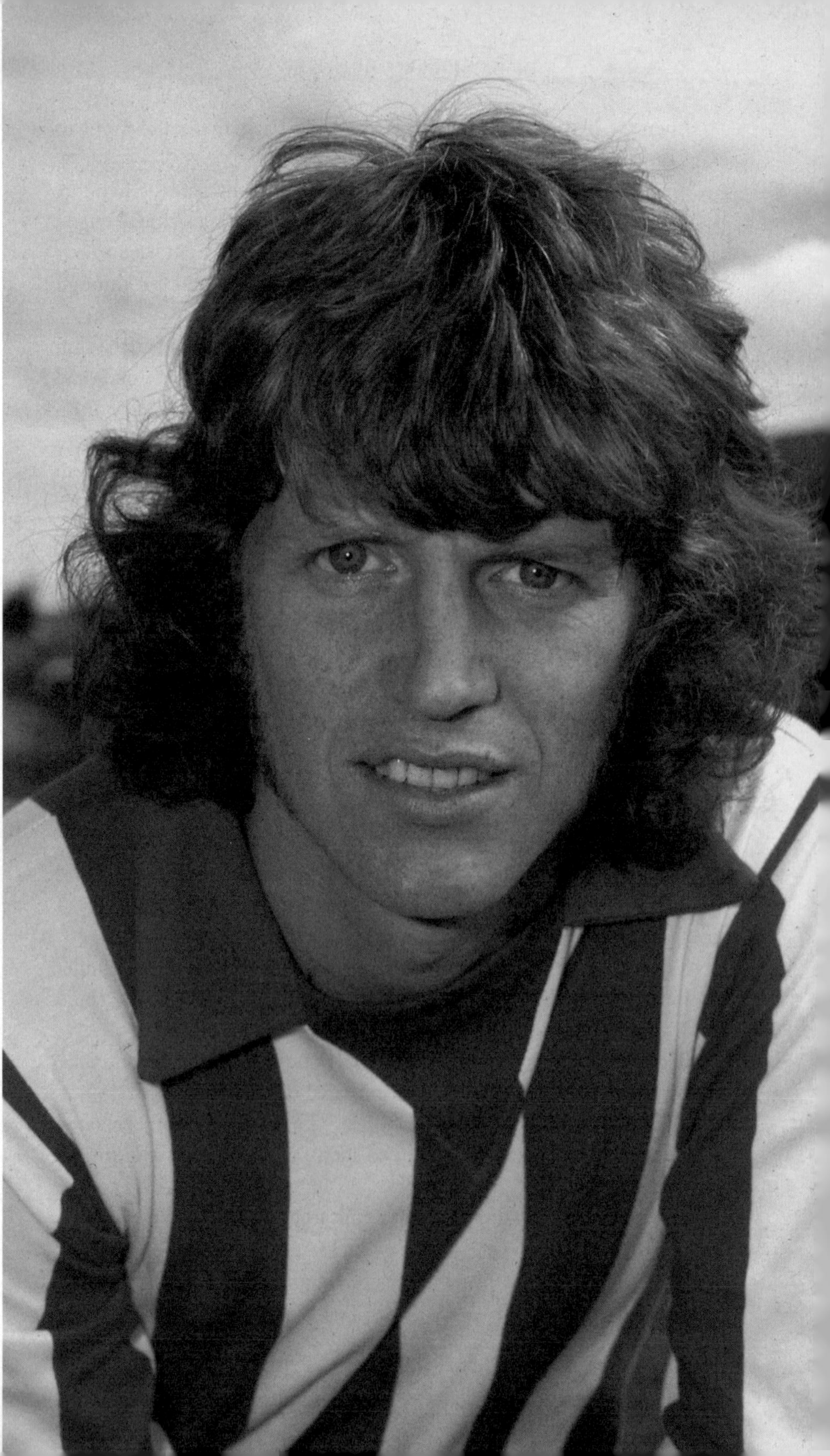

MICK CHANNON

Mick Channon

Southampton 4 (Gilchrist, Channon 3)

West Brom 0

FA Cup fifth round replay
The Dell, Tuesday 17 February 1976

Southampton: Turner, Rodrigues, Blyth, Steele, Peach, Fisher, McCalliog, Holmes, Gilchrist, Channon, Stokes (O'Brien)

WHEN THE final whistle blew after this fantastic performance under the lights at The Dell it was the first time I really felt we had a great chance to go on and win the FA Cup.

Most clubs think they are going to have a good cup run every season but for us we were actually doing it.

I think the whole squad started to believe our name may just be on the trophy that year, especially after the third-round match with Aston Villa when Hughie Fisher rescued us with one minute to go.

Just three days before this fifth-round replay we had made the trip to the Hawthorns, fully confident we could make it three wins out of three against the Baggies after beating them twice in the league already.

But then we hit a problem. On the morning of the Valentine's Day game, four of us woke up with a nasty sickness bug and were serious doubts to make the tie against our second division rivals.

Bobby Stokes, Nick Holmes, Paul Gilchrist and myself were the worst hit by the illness and all of us were big players at the time.

We were already missing Peter Osgood, who was suspended, which made it all the more important we got our big guns out if we wanted to move on to the quarter-finals.

I was an England international closing in on 25 consecutive caps for my country so if myself, and our other stars had not been on the team sheet it would have given them a boost, no doubt about it.

Luckily, there was no social media or Internet in those days so I don't think the opposition really knew we were ill.

We were at the hotel and went to the game with only the people within the club knowing we were not quite right. The decision was made that everyone played and that was that. We got on with it.

I must admit I felt a bit better than Bobby and Nick. I was still suffering but their stomachs were in a worse condition than mine. They were sick, drained and not very well at all.

Nick was probably the fittest bloke at the club at the time and I always remember him trying to make an overlap down the left wing.

I was running with the ball and all I could hear was Nick making a lot of noise trying to run past me. It was hilarious. He must have been very nervous about having an accident.

I turned to him and said, 'What the hell is going on?' I got a mumbled response and as it was only after ten minutes I thought it must be bad if he is really struggling after this point.

There was a lot of talk beforehand that we had gone 12 league and cup games unbeaten so might suffer at the hands of the unlucky number 13. However, I don't think any of the players or staff bought into that nonsense.

We did endure a very long afternoon but more than 10,000 Saints fans who followed us up to the Midlands helped us dig out a 1-1 draw.

I set up Stokesy, who was the closest of any of us to not taking the field, to equalise after Tony Brown had found his way past our keeper Ian Turner to bag the opener.

Of course, those of us who were not fully fit really suffered towards the end and we had to hang on heroically to take the tie back to our place.

West Brom had numerous chances to put us out and probably should have done if I am honest. They would live to regret it.

It is amazing what 72 hours can do as even though it was a very quick turnaround on the Tuesday evening, we were fully recovered, raring to go and everyone was really up for putting on the performance we knew we were capable of.

They were in the same league as us and did not have a bad team at all, very strong and physical. I even recall a certain Bryan Robson coming off the bench at half-time.

Despite our opponents having a good squad and us being relegated from the first division in the 1973/74 season, we had a very good side and I was convinced we would have too much for them.

You could tell, even though we were not playing the strongest sides in the country every week anymore, we were very experienced and had kept our top-flight team pretty much together.

It goes without saying everyone wanted promotion that season but the cup just came along and everyone desperately wanted to win it.

Basically, everything all fitted together nicely for us starting with this match which sticks out vividly for me, not only because I scored a hat-trick, but because it was under the floodlights.

I used to love playing under lights in our old antique of a stadium. It was quite unique and unless you have been there it is hard to explain.

When the supporters stamped on the wooden stand it created a great atmosphere which I never really experienced anywhere else in my career.

The fans were on top of you as the ground was enclosed and intimidating. We will never see the like of it again, it will never be repeated. I feel sorry for the young fans of today who will never know that atmosphere.

It certainly helped the players and other clubs hated coming down. We could beat anyone there and it was always a place where teams could get turned over.

Thanks to the atmosphere and 27,614 people being packed into The Dell, West Brom were certainly not as confident as they were at their place.

And, as I have said already, I loved playing in night matches, but it did pose one slight issue for me; I couldn't undertake my usual pre-match warm-up. On a standard three o'clock kick-off I would have a bowl of cornflakes and some toast before getting my kit on and going to watch the horse racing on a little screen in one of the sponsors' boxes.

It was always a bit tight. I used to be glued to the 2.45pm race before showing a turn of pace to head out onto the pitch with minutes to spare.

I was warmed up and ready to go after that. We had a saying between us senior professionals that the good players don't need a warm-up and the bad ones don't deserve one.

It was obviously very different in those days, compared to all the technical rubbish they seem to have going on today.

On this occasion it didn't do me any harm though as I bagged the opener after only 52 seconds. Maybe I should have done a proper warm-up with the team more often!

It really was a flying start. Pretty much straight from kick-off I picked up a loose ball, took it around one of their players and exchanged a one-two with Stokesy, who repaid the favour from the Saturday to set me up.

Before most of the fans had taken their seats, tucked away their pre-match burger and finished reading the programme I had curled a shot past John Osborne to put us in the lead.

I wasn't expecting to be doing 'the windmill' so early on in the game. My famous celebration did not come from anywhere special, I think it just happened.

We used to play a system in those days that seemed to me to be like a '1-8-1' and when you are up there on your own you are a long way from everyone. It took a while to get back to the halfway line after scoring a goal so I had to occupy the time and when you do a celebration once you are expected to keep it up for ever. So I did.

Sometimes an early goal can throw you off sync and we didn't settle down as quickly as we would have liked.

Johnny Giles's team almost got back on level terms when David Peach didn't get enough on a back pass to Turner and Ally Brown nearly nipped in to capitalise but handled the ball in the process with the goal gaping.

From that moment on though, in an atmosphere that would have been heard across the other side of the city, it was all us and we had the game wrapped up in half an hour.

Funnily enough, when people remember this game it is not my hat-trick that is on everybody's lips, but our second goal from midfielder Gilchrist.

Quite rightly, it is up there with one of The Dell's all-time great goals. Although I bet Gilly couldn't do it again if he tried!

I picked up a pass from our skipper Peter Rodrigues on 17 minutes and touched it on to Stokesy, who saw a shot rebound off a defender.

When it fell to Gilly, who I always felt was under-rated, he controlled the ball in the air, turned, and hit a sublime scissor kick into the roof of the net.

Gilly would go on to score in the semi-final against Crystal Palace with a 25-yard effort to put us into the lead. To this day, I wind him up by maintaining it brushed my sock on the way through and should have been my goal.

Talking of the semi-final, what a memorable day that was for Ossie. Not only did we win to reach his fourth final but he also picked the winner in the Grand National!

Being the horse fanatic if anyone was going to pick the winner it should have been me but I only got third. Typical Ossie.

Back to the West Brom game and I was able to claim my second of the afternoon and our third just before the half-hour mark.

Peach sent a pass through their back-line, which I took up with ease before rounding Osborne to calmly slot home. Cue a deafening roar.

Barring any nightmares we were in the hat for the last eight. After the break, even with a 19-year-old Robson, who looked a tidy player at their disposal, West Brom never really troubled us.

I completed a memorable treble with 15 minutes left after taking a tumble in the box when I was on the receiving end of a shove from defender John Wile trying to get on the end of a cross.

Usually, I never gave it much thought about trying to bag the match ball, but I must have done on this occasion. Jim McCalliog was our usual penalty taker but I didn't even ask him if he would allow me to step up.

In those days no one was going to hand it to me so I just grabbed the ball and took the penalty. Job done.

I didn't score three goals in the same game a huge amount of times as I was more of a match-winner than a prolific striker.

This may sound odd considering I am still the club's all-time leading scorer and topped the scoring charts for five seasons in a row over that period.

Being top scorer is nice but records are there to be broken. Although, with the turnover in players and the way things are now, I think beating my mark of 223 goals might take some doing.

Nobody stays at one club the length of time Matt Le Tissier and I stayed so it will be a challenge to break. When it does get beaten it will be somebody who spends their whole career at Southampton.

I used to score the goals that won the tight games by the odd goal. I could win a game by being in the right place at the right time.

The style of the team we had meant invariably I was on my own at times and my only option was to do something by myself to create a chance, which I enjoyed doing.

Someone like a Steve Moran would be what I consider a real goal-machine who would poach goals most weeks. We were two different types of players.

I played more on the wing or in behind a striker and had a bit of a free role. It was poor old Stokesy who would get all the rubbish jobs to do like chasing back and staying out wide.

Our manager Lawrie McMenemy was pretty good tactically like that. He loved to get on the training ground and get us into shape both physically and from a formation perspective.

He was a huge character was Lawrie and he had to be as it was a massive change when he came in to replace Ted Bates as Ted had been there for so long.

A bit like Ted, Lawrie was a great motivator, very quick-witted and didn't miss a trick. He could put you down with one line or make you feel a million dollars. He was sharp and knew what was required to make the main players tick. It was the change in regime that he had to get into some of my team-mates' heads. Some struggled to adapt and realise it was not Ted's system anymore.

For a few of them it took a bit of time and some of the older players left but my relationship with Lawrie was good, we always got on.

Getting players to perform for him was one of his great strengths. He got the best out of people and that is why he did very well with players like Alan Ball, Ossie and I.

He kept bringing older players in and revitalising them so they would last for another two to three years. Everyone respected him for that.

We played some great stuff and it was a very enjoyable era to be a part of. The 70s were a great time to be football player. With the dodgy haircuts we all had we could have been mistaken for movie stars.

One of the arguments me and Lawrie did have was when I wanted to leave the club in 1975 after we had got relegated the year before.

It was all very different before the Bosman ruling and I was under contract so could not just move on if I wished.

I felt I should have been playing in the top division as at the time I thought it would give me a better chance of continuing my international career and winning some honours.

People were starting to question my England place and despite me being happy at the club the 1974/75 season was so disappointing.

I honestly believed we would win the second division but we had a really bad campaign, finishing 13th.

When I asked for a transfer the club said no as they didn't have any obligation to let me go. There was nothing I could do about it. I had to get on with it.

As I was not particularly happy with the situation Lawrie took the captaincy off me as the player with the armband can't be looking for a move and asking for transfers. That was the way it was.

In the end it was the magical cup run that held us all together for another year and it did surprise us a little considering how poor we had been the season before.

If I hadn't demanded a move I would have been leading the lads up the stairs for the FA Cup Final win and picking up the trophy from the Queen.

That honour fell to Rodrigues, who was a good bloke to have around. He was older than most of us but was very experienced. He had been to the cup final before so knew what it was all about.

But for me the role of captain in football is all a load of rubbish. We had a lot of leaders on the pitch. Peter was the person who had the armband but he only lifted the trophy a few seconds before everyone else.

Peter liked a good bit of banter in the changing room and after the emphatic display over West Brom we no doubt enjoyed a celebratory pint.

In fact, we would socialise after most games whatever the result was. We would be in the pub for sure.

My passion has always been horse racing so a few times some of the lads would follow me along to the races, which were always great days out.

I was never a big gambler or punter. The only times I spent big money on horses was buying them.

The boys were always together. Today they are probably all on their computers checking emails and social media or talking to agents.

We had nothing like that to worry about. We had no one else to talk to except our team-mates, which is probably why we all got on so well.

I think we were a good little unit on and off the pitch. Stokesy was my biggest mate and we spent a fair bit of time together. He was unique in his own way.

We saw plenty of each other and I never found him anything other than great company. He also never drove a car so relied on lifts from me and his wife everywhere!

He would get the train in from Portsmouth every morning and be at the ground for 8am. If he missed the last train he would stay at mine and help me muck out the stables in the morning.

Like myself, Stokesy was also being talked about for a move and came very close to joining our fierce rivals Pompey earlier in the season of the FA Cup win. Thank God he did not!

To have a mix of characters in any side is important and we certainly had that in abundance during our cup winning triumph.

Most players were not frightened to speak their minds. For sure you have quieter people but no one backed down, especially not me. If something had to be said I would say it, as would Jim Steele who always had plenty to say.

I have lost count of the amount of times there would be arguments in the changing rooms at half-time and Lawrie struggled to get a word in edgeways.

Everyone knew where the line was though and that came from our days in the academy when we were brought up in the correct way.

Starting out as a young player for me it came down to a choice between joining Southampton or Swindon. The decision was not based on financial incentives but purely that I had been to the club a lot as a youngster.

My father was a Southampton man and passed his love for Saints onto me. I used to go and watch games and that is what swung it.

As I am a local lad that gave me an instant bond and connection with the fans. I think me being a striker also helped as the goalscorer, more often than not in my case, gave them something to cheer about.

I was close to joining Swindon but Ted came in at the last minute and said he wanted me on the south coast. The rest is history.

The club gives everyone a chance and that was the big attraction. There have been so many great players including guys I would look up to like Terry Paine and John Sydenham.

To win the cup for your hometown club is a dream come true. There were only really two competitions if you weren't in Europe so that made it all the more special. But once we did not get promoted the following season, despite playing in the European Cup Winners' Cup, I knew it was time to make a move.

I couldn't wait around for ever. I was getting towards the later stages of my career and agreed a £300,000 move to Manchester City. It was a no-brainer and I had to try something else.

Once again I was on the back pages of every newspaper, seemingly going to every big club in the country for huge amounts of money.

But Southampton was always a home for me and always will be. It was where all my family, friends and horses were and I struggled to settle.

Funnily enough a couple of years later I came back and had some more great times with the likes of Kevin Keegan and Ball.

I am not one who reminisces a huge amount but it is the whole FA Cup run and final victory that I look back on most fondly in my career.

They were great days and I enjoyed them so much. I had lots of good people around me who it was a pleasure to share the pitch with. Football was a way of life for me and never an occupation.

My hat-trick against West Brom turned out to be very important. The fact I could play such a big part in Southampton's greatest ever triumph gives me a feeling of pride I may never experience again.

Well, unless I train a Grand National winner.

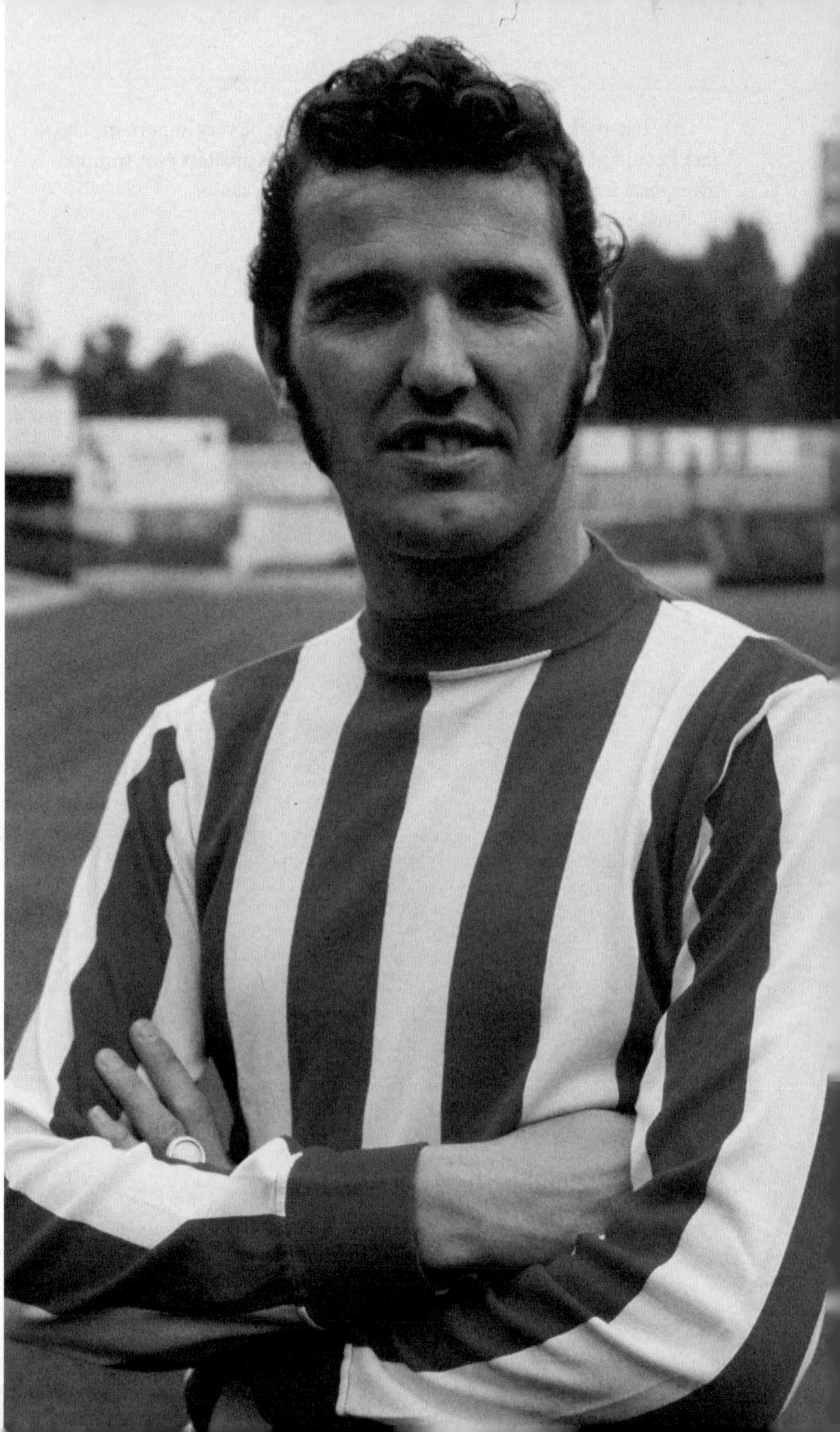

TERRY PAINE

Terry Paine

Leyton Orient 1 (Allan)

Southampton 1 (Paine)

League Division Two
Brisbane Road, Monday 9 May 1966

Southampton: Forsyth, Webb, Hollywood, White, Knapp, Walker, Paine, Chivers, Dean, Melia, Sydenham

HAVING PLAYED 815 games for Southampton it is not an easy task to single out just one but when you look back on this game at Brisbane Road the goal I scored to bring top-flight football to the city for the first time has to go down as the most important in our history.

I believe it was the moment that helped shape Saints' future and transform the club into the one we all know and love so many decades later.

From what Southampton were then and where they are now, the foundations were built by our second division promotion-winning team and the great Ted Bates.

The club had suffered a massive disappointment six years earlier when, after being eight points clear and looking certainties for promotion, they somehow managed to blow it.

At the time the feeling in the local area was they bottled it because they did not want to go up and that it was too big a step.

That was a stigma that stayed with the club and hung around for a long time, but the real truth was they lost their great goalscorer Charlie Wayman to injury at a critical time of the season and never recovered from that.

I am sure some of our supporters were dreading a similar collapse as they made their way to east London by the coachload but the players were determined we would not be remembered as another team of nearly-men.

The expectations had been very high going into the game as we were on a ten-match unbeaten run and 12,000 people travelled by road and rail – and I am sure by pushbike if they had to.

It was a remarkable turnout and after the final whistle, as we were carried off the pitch on the shoulders of our fans as heroes, it felt like there were 50,000 of them, all resplendent in red and white.

Ted had put his faith in the youth team and built from there and how he was rewarded.

That promotion also heralded the start of an amazing climb through the leagues, and to go from the old Division Three into the first division and into Europe under Ted's expert guidance was a phenomenal achievement.

With so much money flooding through the game now since the advent of the Premier League, I doubt it will be possible for any lower league team to complete such a rise again.

By the time the Orient game came around, Manchester City – who had the great Mike Summerbee and Colin Bell in their line-up – had already won the title so the best we could hope for was second place and Coventry were pushing us hard.

We had to go to City on the final day but knew a draw against Orient would mean we were promoted barring a freak six-goal defeat at Maine Road. It was Orient's last game of the season and the home side were determined to put on a show to send their supporters away for the summer happy and upset our promotion dream in the process.

We got off to a bad start and when we fell behind after just seven minutes I'm sure the nerves were jangling in the away end, especially after what had happened a few years earlier.

Campbell Forsyth had already been called into action early on when Orient's record appearance holder Peter Allen raced through and finished coolly past our Scottish goalkeeper.

The good thing about going behind so early was we had plenty of time to get back into the match and our players kept their cool and composure, believing we would get chances if we just kept playing the same free-flowing football we had produced all season.

Sure enough Jimmy Melia caused a scramble in the Orient goal and Norman Dean put a header over after I had whipped in a free kick.

We had a let-off when David Methick, the Orient striker, beat our offside trap but thankfully he made a mess of his shot and lashed the ball over the crossbar.

That miss felt like a turning point in the game and so it proved seven minutes into the second half when a long punt upfield from Forsyth bought his opposite number Victor Rouse charging off his line.

Orient defender Gordon Ferry tried to head the ball back to Rouse but his effort was never going to reach its intended target.

I was the closest Saints player to the ball and I knew if I timed my run correctly I would get there first so I waited until I could see the whites of Rouse's eyes and calmly nodded the ball past him.

I kept my eye on the ball and everything dropped perfectly for me. It beat a couple of defenders in mid-flight and bounced nicely for me to pop it into the unguarded net.

The memory of that goal will stay with me forever and is documented in every book I read about Southampton.

The goal also stands out because I did not score many headers in my career. In fact I can count the ones I did get on one hand. I remember another famous one against Manchester United in an FA Cup tie but that is about it.

I wasn't the biggest of players and not a particularly good header of the ball. In those days it spent quite a lot of time in the air and the defenders really attacked the ball well.

Heading really was an art and you left if to those who made it their speciality. Players like Ron Davies, who was brilliant in the air and would always stick it in the back of the net. I remember Ron once scored all four goals in a 4-1 win at Man United, prompting the legendary Sir Matt Busby to call him the best centre-forward in Europe.

The balls were heavy as lead too and that put me off heading them. I never even used to go in the wall to defend free kicks because if one hit you, especially if it had been raining, it would leave an imprint of the manufacturer's logo.

They retained water and I have seen many a player knocked out. The skill factor of players back then was so high to be able to play in those kind of conditions it makes you wonder how today's 'superstars' would cope.

There was a bit of apprehension about the place all the time Orient had the lead but the frustration quickly fell away once we equalised and our travelling army went wild in the stands. They didn't stop singing for ten minutes solid.

After my goal went it we still felt we could go on and win the game but didn't create many clear-cut scoring chances as the match became pretty cagey.

Martin Chivers did force one save from Rouse but Orient were happy to take a draw from a side on their way to promotion, so we knew the result was not going to do us any harm.

We were on a really good run of wins coming into the game and while we knew City would probably win it we also felt the runners-up spot was ours for the taking.

Coventry were hot on our heels but I never felt there was any real doubt we would make it. However to say that and to actually see the job through are two very different things.

As Saints fans knew from bitter experience getting over the line is never easy and that, I think, is why there was so much emotion at the end of the game, because of the realisation we had finally done it.

Our fans spilling onto the pitch in their thousands from all four sides of the ground and carrying us all the way to the tunnel was an amazing spectacle.

Although some of our loyal followers were a bit too keen as they started to clamber onto the field when the referee blew for a throw-in, mistaking it for the final whistle, and had to be sent back to their seats.

It is a shame in those days there were not so many cameras at grounds outside the bigger clubs because it would have made great TV.

The only other exodus of supporters I can remember on a similar scale was an FA Cup tie against Nottingham Forest when we beat them 5-0 at White Hart Lane after drawing with them twice.

All we saw on the motorway driving from Southampton up to the capital were streams of headlights and the queues to get into the ground were so bad some of our fans never made it to their seats until the second half had kicked off.

On this occasion it was obvious during and after the game our supporters vastly outnumbered Orient fans and at full time it was absolute pandemonium.

They were great scenes of us being smothered by the crowd and the champagne was flowing in the dressing room afterwards as the club directors came down to congratulate us.

We all celebrated except Ted. We all begged him to indulge in a glass or two of bubbly but he sternly refused to join the celebrations until after the City game, once it was mathematically impossible for us to be caught.

That was typical Ted; professional to the last and always keeping a steady head even when all around him, including his bosses, were losing theirs.

We still had a job to do in the City game but after holding Joe Mercer's side, who would go on to be crowned champions of England only two seasons later, to a goalless draw the time for partying could really begin.

We got welcomed home by the mayor of Southampton and loads of fans had crammed into the city's central train station waiting for our train to pull in to the platform.

The nice thing about going by train was that we got to mingle with the supporters and anyone could walk down to our carriage for a friendly chat.

As a result there was a nice bond between the players on the pitch and the punters on the terraces. We chatted together, met people and became friendly with fans because they were on many of the same away trips as we were.

We had some great lads in the team like Forsyth, the man who made my famous goal. He was a top shot stopper and a great guy.

I played against him for England against Scotland at Hampden Park in one of the now defunct home internationals. We got beat 1-0 and that didn't go down well when we returned to club training.

We also had George O'Brien. He was a prolific scorer and great finisher. George was my right wing partner so I was as close to him as any of my other team-mates.

George was a dour Scotsman with a very dry sense of humour. He was also a good golfer whom Ted got from Leeds for a paltry amount.

He had a dodgy knee that flared up after every game so we wouldn't see him at training until the following Friday.

Then there was Ken Wimshurst who played at inside-forward and was on the brink of the England team, David Burnside who Ted picked up from West Bromwich Albion and Melia, who had spent most of his career at Liverpool and was an ever-present in our first season after winning promotion.

Ted had a brilliant eye for a player, that was his biggest strength and he would go and watch a target eight or nine times before signing him.

I loved his management style because he always knew when was the right time to put his arm round your shoulder and when was the right time to give you a rollicking.

He was a very fair man and he appreciated the players he had and what they were doing for the club. I think that was why he was able to build winning teams

He taught us never to worry too much about the opposition and always encouraged us to concentre on what we were good at.

I cannot even remember what he said to us in the team talk before the Orient game but it would have been very simple because there were no dossiers on opponents compiled back then.

I cannot speak highly enough of Ted. You don't stay at a club for 60-odd years and become 'Mr Southampton' as he did without being special.

He was the main reason I stayed at Southampton for as long as I did because the truth is before our promotion I had been tempted to leave.

Clubs were interested in me and like anybody ambitious I wanted to play in the top league but that promotion win curbed my interest in moving onto a bigger club.

It seemed every time I got itchy feet we got promoted so I didn't have an argument, not that Ted would have ever let me go anyway.

I was dying to go that summer of 1966 before being part of England's World Cup winning squad. Tottenham were the front runners to take me and I was playing with Jimmy Greaves at international level so it seemed a logical move to make.

Harry Evans, the Spurs assistant manager, was at all our games and it was a case of tapping you on the shoulder after a match.

He'd be stood there winking at me and asking me to put in a transfer request.

But John Barber, the Saints chairman, called me in to tell me under no circumstances would I be allowed to move. That deflated me.

Spurs were a massive club and were doing the business in the 60s under Bill Nicholson's management so to be thought of in the same breath was unbelievable.

Greaves was chatting me up every time we went away with England, saying 'why didn't you move?'

I was also linked with Manchester United and Liverpool because I was doing well and scoring goals in Division Two, had got into the England team and scored a hat-trick at Wembley against Northern Ireland in an 8-3 win.

I went to the World Cup with England having never kicked a ball in the top flight which was unheard of, so I was the one everyone looked at.

But maybe the grass is always greener on the other side until you get there and had I moved I would not have gone on to achieve my record appearances for Southampton, which is something I am very proud of.

With the regularity modern players swap clubs I think that record will stand for a long time to come.

The first time I crossed paths with Ted was when I joined the Saints youth team and I found him the nicest, most charming man I had met.

He was a football man through and through and lived and breathed the game.

He had a great belief in youth, which served the club well over the years and he gave me and countless others the opportunity to make it in the first-team where other managers would have been reluctant.

He was ahead of his time in that respect and saw changes had to be made in order for the club to move forward.

In the second season I was there he sacked 15 senior players and from the youth team I played in 12 of us turned professional. That was an extraordinary amount of players.

We had a great basis of young talent but, as I have already said, Ted tinkered in the transfer market too and that gave us an enviable blend of youth and experience.

I joined the youth scheme at the same time as Colin Holmes, a Winchester boy like me, who made one first team experience at Wrexham and went on to be a journeyman around Hampshire. I was at school with him as well.

We also had John Sydenham, a terrific player who made over 400 appearances for Saints and played on the opposite wing to me, Peter Vine, Terry Simpson, who went on to join West Brom and Wesley Maughan, an Isle of Wight lad who played league football for Reading.

The whole club was run on a shoe string in those days, and the youth set-up was nothing like the academy that would go on to become the envy of the whole of Europe, but it more than proved its worth with the number of players coming through.

I was playing for Winchester City in the Hampshire League when I was spotted by Saints. Our manager Harry Osman held the scoring record of 21 goals in a season before I went on to break it.

By then I had already had trials at Portsmouth and Arsenal so the word was out I was making progress.

A pal of mine called Ted and said, 'You better get your backside in gear if you want this lad.'

He invited Colin, who had also been on trial at Arsenal, and I to meet him at his office at 2pm the following afternoon and as we walked in he locked the door behind us.

He wanted us to sign amateur forms. We kept saying we were going back to Arsenal as we had both been invited to a final trial at Highbury.

Eventually about 4pm we were starving hungry and wanted to go and get our tea so we signed the forms just so he would unlock the door.

I later discovered there had been a mix-up at Arsenal after the first trial when they should have sent me forms to sign so I guess the Gunners' loss was Saints' gain.

Ted was an FA man, who had coached at Lilleshall and at the time English coaches were the be all and end all.

He was a highly qualified coach with limited resources. We had to scrape and borrow footballs just so we had something to use in training and had to keep the best ball for the game at the weekend when we were due to play at home.

It was not uncommon to use the same ball for three or four games in a row so the equipment was pretty basic.

Among Ted's other discoveries were Mick Channon, who went on to become one of the greatest finishers in England, and Derek Reeves who broke the Football League scoring record in Division Three. I always associated myself with good goalscorers.

We started to grow as a team and with Ted at the helm attracted players to the club. Cliff Huxford, who is also featured in this book, was our captain for a long time and was a fabulous servant for Saints.

Ted produced players of quality and strength but was also shrewd enough to realise when we needed strengthening as we progressed up the divisions.

There was no real money so we relied on Bill Etherington, our scout, to spot the players.

Ted did not have a big back-room team to rely on. There was him, Jimmy Gallagher the physio and a reserve team manager. There was nobody else.

The process of getting into the top flight was slower than I wanted but once we got there and achieved that the next big step was survival.

The fact we managed to make it all the way to Europe was quite remarkable for a club of our size and that could never have happened without Ted and that manic Monday at Orient.

CLIFF HUXFORD

Cliff Huxford

Southampton 5 (Reeves 5)

Leeds 4 (Peyton, McCole, Charlton, Cameron)

League Cup Fourth Round
The Dell, Monday 5 December 1960

Southampton: Reynolds, Davies, Traynor, Conner, Page, Huxford, Paine, O'Brien, Reeves, Mulgrew, Sydenham

IT MAY seem strange that despite a successful spell as captain, more than 300 appearances for Southampton and two promotions at the club, my favourite game is one where I let in four goals while playing as a makeshift goalkeeper.

What drama. Add to that the floodlights going out twice causing 62 minutes of delays in total and Derek Reeves scoring a last-gasp winner, his FIFTH of the match, you can see why it is a match that lives long in the memory.

Leaving the pitch surrounded by a host of Saints fans trying to hold me aloft after they had invaded from the stands was something I will never forget.

I have always been brave on the pitch and never shirked a challenge that came my way. That is why when our goalkeeper Ron Reynolds was stretched off after 20 minutes with a bad wrist and back injury I had no doubts about agreeing to step in between the sticks.

Despite never playing in goal before I thought I could do a decent job. How hard could it be? Very, was the answer as I would later find out.

Terry Paine was our usual reserve goalkeeper but our manager Ted Bates had made the call to leave Terry up front. What a masterstroke that turned out to be with our number seven going on to create all five goals. By the time I was called upon we were already one-nil up and had endured one floodlight failure. After ten minutes, with the scores goalless, we became ghostly shadows to the 13,000 fans in the stands when everything pitched into darkness.

Electricians quickly tried to solve the problem while the players kept warm by passing the ball around and doing some shooting practice before finally relenting and heading for the warmth of the dressing rooms.

If I had known what was to follow I would have gone in goal for some much needed practice as well!

The crowd roared when, 28 minutes later and after what seemed like an eternity, the lights above us flooded the ground once again.

We started the stronger of the two sides and got our noses in front soon after the restart when Terry whipped in a pinpoint cross which Derek firmly headed past Alan Humphreys for his first goal.

After the restart though Ron, who often made saves I thought were impossible, dived at the feet of Leeds striker John McCole and suffered a horrendous looking injury to his wrist and back

These were tough times and as there were no substitutes if you had a one per cent chance of staying on, you would do it, so we all knew he was in a real state. In hospital it was discovered Ron had broken a bone in his back and was out of action for four weeks.

It was down to me to pull on the green jersey and initially I didn't mind as it was warmer than my usual match shirt and being a cold December night it came in handy. But after keeping net for only a couple of minutes we plunged into darkness once again and this time, the novelty had worn off, and everyone was starting to get very annoyed.

We didn't hang around on the pitch and retreated to the changing rooms again. Some of the lads were smoking cigarettes to warm themselves up and there was a bit of laughter flying around at how I may perform as a number one.

It was a game we really wanted to win. It is true, our opponents had been relegated to join us in the second division a year earlier but they still had plenty of top players like Billy Bremner at their disposal.

We had lost 4-2 at home in the league to them in September and would go on to lose 3-0 at Elland Road later in the season, but we did manage to finish above them in the table.

That did not happen very much afterwards as we all know the force they later became when Don Revie took over three months after this tie.

Despite heavy criticism from some of the bigger clubs we thought the newly-formed League Cup was a great idea and loved the competition.

It was in its first year and with a quarter-final spot at stake we desperately wanted to progress and had experienced a few dramas and scalps on the way already.

In the first round it took three matches in total and two replays to see off Newport County. Obviously the format has changed now but in that first year you kept playing 90 minutes until somebody won.

After then seeing off Colchester United, we knocked out Liverpool at Anfield in the third round which really made us think we could go all the way but we eventually went out to Burnley. When we finally returned to the action after a 34-minute delay with ten men and a centre-back in goal, taking our place in the last eight looked unlikely.

I say ten men, it was more like nine as George O'Brien was really struggling and could barely walk but stayed on to make up the numbers.

We were aided by our opponents also suffering a knee injury to their full-back Alf Jones, although he hobbled on until early in the second half so they were effectively down to ten as well.

What happened next was hard to believe. I was expecting a bombardment of crosses, shots and high balls to try and trouble me but they never arrived.

If Jack Taylor's side had been sloppy and slow out of the blocks after the first delay, this time around they were even worse.

Terry was scintillating on the night and our opponents could not get near him. Terry, who scored both our goals in the win over Liverpool I have mentioned already, was an old-fashioned winger.

He was well on the way to receiving his first England call-up which would see him play in the 1966 World Cup finals. He was a different class to most of his second division opponents, and no one could cope with him.

John Sydenham had the pace and Terry had the skill. They were our two main men in the side and obviously Derek chipped in with some goals as well but was not as consistent.

Twice before the break Terry got into good positions to put the ball on a plate for Derek, who gratefully snapped up the chances to seal his treble and put us into a commanding 3-0 lead before we headed for the dressing room once more.

We started like a train after half-time and the Paine–Reeves combination came to fruition once more with Derek putting us 4-0 up after 50 minutes. Job done, or so we thought.

It was getting embarrassing for Leeds now but when Jones finally gave in and left the pitch for good it seemed to galvanise his team-mates.

The Lilywhites put on a devastating 17-minute spell to pull themselves right back in the game. Noel Payton, John McCole and Jack Charlton all scored with shots I could do nothing about.

Charlton was forgetting his defensive duties and was playing so high up the pitch I was surprised he did not get a nosebleed.

On 79 minutes he was upended in the box and despite my protest the referee pointed to the spot.

I was starting to not enjoy my new role. Being in goal is great when you are 4-0 up as you can just stand back and watch the boys play.

But standing on the goal line about to face a penalty after letting three quick-fire goals in was a bit of a nightmare.

I came very close to stopping Bobby Cameron's effort but to no avail and the scores were level. Poor Derek must have been thinking what more do I need to do to win a game of football?

After seeing four goals fly past me you might be mistaken for thinking all I could catch was a cold on this winter evening but at 4-4 I made two vital saves to keep us in the game.

The interceptions laid the foundations for us to go up the other end and score with only 25 seconds remaining.

Terry dazzled and tricked his way up the field before setting Derek free with a defence-splitting pass. Derek, showing boundless energy, sprinted after it and beat Humphreys with a crisp right-footed shot.

I jumped for joy back in my goal and when the final whistle went, two hours and 40 minutes after kick-off, I had to glance at the scoreboard to check we had actually won. What a game.

Goalkeeper was not the role Ted had envisaged for me when he signed me from Chelsea as a 22-year-old but this would not be the final time he would put me behind the defence. I would go on to do it a further three times in my eight-year career on the south coast.

I originally arrived as the replacement for Charlie Livesey, who went the other way to Stamford Bridge, with my new club also receiving a £12,000 fee.

Those were big shoes to fill but Terry later said I was one of Ted's 'shrewdest ever signings' as the money was well spent on Dick Connor and George O'Brien.

Dick was the footballer between us and I was the ball winner. We were a very good pair and knew each other's games down to a tee.

Ted came to watch me play and liked what he saw. Managers were more hands-on then and the transfer would have been sorted out over a pint after the match. No agents or anything.

Chelsea had signed me straight from the Army as an 18-year-old. Funnily enough my year-and-a-half stint of national service took place in Netley, near Southampton. Little did I know I would end up back in the area permanently.

While serving my time in the Army, on day releases, I would go and watch the club and stand behind the goals at The Dell.

The crowd were on top of you and I thought, yeah, I would like to play here one day. It was an electric atmosphere.

Southampton may have even watched me play Army football as I took part in a lot of games, sometimes on a pitch I had just prepared as I was a groundsman.

When the time came to leave Chelsea all I was concerned about was playing first team football. Ted assured me and guaranteed me that.

He was convinced we had plenty of footballers but needed someone to stamp their authority on games. He chose me and I was happy to oblige.

I think he wanted a strong character in the changing room as well. For players like myself, who had been in the Army, we were strong-minded and tough as we had to be.

I was on an £18-a-week contract which was not awful money. That was the pretty standard wage at the club and I was happy to receive it. It provided me the opportunity to live comfortably off the pitch.

When I signed I had no idea I would last for so long and be such a success but I was just what they wanted, the last piece of the jigsaw.

Ted was the manager for my whole period at the club. He was football mad and we got on well. I was the first name on the team sheet.

He was a good leader of men and we would all run through a brick wall for him if asked. He had an ambition for Southampton to take us to greater heights and thanks to his desire and hard work he made it come true.

In my eyes he was the best manager to get us out of Division Three and up to the top flight. Tactically he had us well drilled.

He would not lose his temper much either and his idea was to talk us through our mistakes and be calm rather than scream and shout at us. If at half-time we were behind he would always have a strategy to get us back in the game.

Ted assembled a fantastic mix of skilful players and strong hard men. We fitted together very well indeed and it made it hard for other teams to work us out as they didn't know how to approach us.

Terry, Derek and Tommy Mulgrew were all very good football players but were a different type to other players of that generation as they were elegant and skilful.

I was a ball winner but I was never worried any of the players would be too lightweight to handle themselves.

Sydenham was a fantastic player. He used to let them have the ball and lull them into a false sense of security and then all of a sudden, bang, put in a big tackle.

Maybe Painey off the ball couldn't hurt a fly but on the ball he was a genius. It was a very good team and one I was proud to lead.

When I left Chelsea one of the things that inspired me was that I felt I had to prove a point. That was the way I used to think and motivate myself. I was thinking 'why always me' way before Mario Balotelli unveiled his famous T-shirt.

When I was sold from Chelsea, why me? When things happened on the pitch, why me? In the end I proved to my former employers I was good enough to be a professional footballer.

In our first season I was quickly handed the captaincy and we won the third division, getting promoted up to Division Two. Talk about making an impression.

I was surprised but honoured to get the captaincy at the time as I was all mouth on the pitch and maybe sometimes did not set the best example with my colourful language.

This may have been why I never got an England call-up. I never thought I would get one because of the type of player I was, my face would not fit with the Three Lions.

Make no mistake though, I was not the only one dishing out some verbals. My opponents would give it back to me, and Leeds were always very good at that. It was always a game-and-a-half.

In the dressing room I was a lot quieter though and the only routine we had was for Ted to get up and give his team talk. I would never stand up and give any opinions or words of advice. I did my talking on the pitch.

The board were a bit uneasy about giving me the armband and they wanted Terry to be the captain as he had played 100 more games than me and was two years older.

Some of the senior professionals, like Terry, did not make life especially easy for me. Players were going behind my back and talking to Ted about things without me knowing.

Sydenham and Terry were in the youth team together so were very close and backed each other to the hilt.

As soon as I found out what was going on I packed it in. It made for a difficult environment in the dressing room for a short period of time and I did feel let down.

I would say one thing and the manager would say another. I couldn't be doing with that and gave up the armband after two years.

Even when I was captain I was always a bit of a loner. There was not one player I was especially close to and I distanced myself from the lads. In fact, only two or three would socialise together outside of football.

We would go our separate ways which was unusual in that era. On the pitch we would unite furiously and be a close-knit group but afterwards we didn't go to the pub or go dancing or anything.

We would go to the bar at the stadium and socialise with our opponents and some of the supporters but not for very long.

I would only ever have one, maybe two beers, and then go home. There was not a drinking culture at the club as Ted would not have allowed it. He was not a big drinker, or at least we never saw it. We all needed a few drinks after this game against Leeds though, I certainly did!

Without the stresses and pressures of captaincy I could just focus on playing and really got back to enjoying it again.

What I most enjoyed was the physical side of things and I was a hard nut. Ron 'Chopper' Harris was in the youth set-up at Chelsea when I made my debut and he has since listed me as a tougher player than himself.

It was a very physical time and Leeds was always a rough game. It was on the edge of being quite nasty.

I would embrace the challenges though and get stuck right in. If a Premier League player of today played in one of these matches they would not know what had hit them.

I think it would also be interesting to see a modern referee have a go trying to keep one of our games in hand.

I am not proud to say I broke a few players' legs in my career, although not on purpose I would like to add.

Despite all this I never really had any fights and don't ever remember getting a red card, plenty of yellows mind. I dread to think what a red card offence would have been!

I always used to play the ball and not the player, but I was aggressive. If a player got hit while I got the ball then so be it.

Centre-forwards were scared of me. The Leeds front three of McCole, Peyton and Colin Grainger were as well, I could see it in their eyes. That gave me a great sensation and I knew I had won the battle before the game even started.

It was not just opponents on my radar, when new players joined the club I would kick them up in the air in their first training session. I was just as physical in training as I was in a match situation.

In some conditions we would train in the car park of The Dell if the pitch was not suitable for use. It was very hard on your knees and joints. I remember aching so much after.

It was old fashioned but sometimes using jumpers for goalposts would bring out a sense of being a kid again and I don't remember anyone moaning about it. We did what we had to do.

We would also use the public common just past the cricket ground a lot as well as we did not have any training pitches of our own.

It hardened us up and made us appreciate much more playing on a grass pitch. On the rock solid Tarmac we didn't wear football boots but rubber studs and even I would not slide tackle.

As much I loved The Dell, training in the car park was not its best feature. My debut was against Norwich in 1959 and I instantly knew it was the perfect place for me.

It suited me and my style right down to the ground. Intense atmosphere, tight ground, and always packed to the rafters.

To this day I have no idea how they managed to fit 30,000 people inside. It was so over-populated, too many fans for the seats. Opposing players were intimidated even before I had got hold of them.

We didn't lost many games at The Dell. We would be so pumped up, as in the changing room beforehand, all you could hear was noise above you.

When you went down the stairs to the tunnel, wow, the wall of noise hit you in the face when you went out onto the pitch.

Being at the front of the line-up it would reach me first and I couldn't help but smile on the inside. Leading the lads out was one of my favourite parts of the day.

This team more or less stayed together and got promoted up to the first division in 1966, which was a great achievement by all at the club.

Unfortunately it was the beginning of the end for me and I was transferred to Exeter City in 1967 after only one season in the big time.

Just like when I arrived, I had no choice in the matter. It was very sad as I felt like I had been on so much of a journey with the club. I desperately wanted to continue.

In the end it may have been something to do with me opening my mouth once too often.

But I have many happy memories from this era and period of my life as we were winning games regularly. I like to think I contributed greatly to our success.

Hampshire is my home and I still have a great affection for the area. I follow the team as much as I can and it gives me a spring in my step when I hear they have won.

I suppose you could say Southampton and I fitted like a glove. If only I had had a better pair on the night Derek Reeves saved my blushes after letting in four in a match that at the time was recorded as one of the best in football history.